The Ragged Trousered Philanthrop

Robert Tressell's **The Ragged Trou**
group of painters and decorators a
complacent and stagnating Edward.
classic of working-class literature since its first publication in 1914.
This brilliant stage version by Stephen Lowe, the author of
Touched, was first seen in 1978, when Joint Stock Theatre
Company toured the country playing to packed houses. The play
was revived in 1983 at the Half Moon Theatre, London, in the wake
of the recent General Election, and again in 1991 for a touring
production by the Birmingham Rep.

Stephen Lowe's plays include **Comic Pictures** (Scarborough, 1976);
Sally Ann Hallelujah Band (Nottingham Playhouse Theatre
Roundabout, 1977); **Touched** (Nottingham Playhouse, 1977; Royal
Court Theatre, 1981; joint winner of the George Devine Award);
The Ragged Trousered Philanthropists (Joint Stock Theatre
Company, 1978; Half Moon, London, 1983; Birmingham Rep.,
1991); **Glasshouses** (Royal Court Theatre Upstairs, 1981); **Tibetan
Inroads** (Royal Court Theatre, 1981); **Moving Pictures** (Royal
Court Theatre, 1981); **Seachange** (Riverside Studios, 1984);
Keeping Body and Soul Together (Royal Court Theatre Upstairs,
1984); **Divine Gossip** (Royal Shakespeare Company's The Pit,
1988); and **Paradise** (Nottingham Playhouse, 1990). He has
translated Ostrovsky's **The Storm** for the RSC and Schiller's
William Tell for the Sheffield Crucible. He is also the editor for
Methuen's series of **Peace Plays**.

Methuen New Theatrescripts series offers frontline intelligence of the most original and exciting work from the fringe:

The Ragged Trousered Philanthropists

A Play by
Stephen Lowe

based on the novel by Robert Tressell

To Fred Ball,
and to Joint Stock
for their work

Methuen Drama

A Methuen New Theatrescript

First published in Great Britain in 1978 by the Joint Stock Theatre Company. This revised edition published in 1983 by Methuen London Ltd. Reprinted in 1991 by Methuen Drama, Michelin House, 81 Fulham Road, London SW3 6RB and distributed in the United States of America by HEB Inc, 361 Hanover Street, Portsmouth, New Hampshire, NH 03801 3959.

Copyright © 1978, 1983 by Stephen Lowe.

This adaptation has been made by arrangement with Lawrence and Wishart Ltd, publishers of the first complete edition of **The Ragged Trousered Philanthropists**.

ISBN 0-413-54400-1

A CIP catalogue record for this book is available from the British Library.

Printed and bound in Great Britain
by Cox & Wyman Ltd

Is **The Ragged Trousered Philanthropists** simply an interesting piece of social and political history? Or is it relevant to life in the 1990s?

It's tempting to feel that the world depicted in the play, and the novel, is today a historical curiosity, a benchmark of how far we've come in industrial relations and social conditions.

People do not starve when they lose their jobs. The backstreets of our industrial towns and cities are no longer full of rickety and malnourished children. Corrupt individuals and businessmen have ceased to hold the power of life and death over the families in their employ. The existence of the Welfare State has changed all of that. Hasn't it? If we fall sick, we turn to the NHS. If we're made redundant there is income support, child benefit, funeral grants, the Social Fund, rent allowance. We are cared for from 'cradle to grave'. Aren't we?

Well, up to a point, Lord Copper. For millions, life in the 1990s is anything but cushioned. In the play, the ragged trousered philanthropists spend all their time working or seeking work. The thing they fear above all else is unemployment. For them no wage means no food. Throughout the 1980s, also, the spectre of redundancy has dominated millions of homes. Many of our industrial towns have been turned into wastelands. As the new recession deepens, unemployment will rise again above 2 million. The result no longer is starvation, but it is poverty and humiliation. Families are separated as people seek work down South, and anyone who has travelled on one of the Sunday night 'Tebbit Expresses' will be in no doubt about the misery caused by such a life.

In the novel **The Ragged Trousered Philanthropists**, the death of Philpott is caused by the use of shoddy and unfit tools and the need to save time and money skimping on safety procedures. He falls from a ladder when the safety mechanism fails to support him. Last year people died on building sites in London at the rate of one a week, which is hardly surprising when the 4000 plus sites were supervised by just 12 inspectors, following Government cuts in the Health and Safety Commission. Indeed, during the 1980s, out of the 1.5 million working in industry, 1500 were killed, while 40,000 died from industrially related diseases. The Health and Safety Executive's own report, 'Blackspot Construction', said 70% of these fatal accidents could have been prevented by management action. But while fines for negligence are so laughably low, with an average of £361 per offence between 1985 and 1987, it's not surprising that many firms invest little in safety. As a result, Philpott dies again, three times every week.

Owen's description of the need to levy a rate in Mugsborough seems depressingly apt. Owen's argument, in the age of the Poll Tax, is that a ha'penny rate would mean that the Mugsborough Corporation could ensure that none of its children went hungry, but of course the people who count in the town prefer not to do that. They instead spend their time in charitable works for the 'dear little children'. Naturally the charitable giving helps, but only to a point. Many are missed out, or excluded by means testing. There is a clear echo of the present Government law of social policy – 'charity is both virtuous and sufficient', 'people should give what they want to', 'it is not the job of the state to provide'. Private charity is replacing public provision, now as then.

The difference is, today we can always complain about it in our liberal democracy, proud of the freedom of its press and media. Can't we? In **The Ragged Trousered Philanthropists**, all the Mugsborough papers are owned by a monopoly, unlike today when we've got Murdoch *and* Maxwell *and* Conrad Black . . . In fact, outside of Mugsborough, in Tressell's day every major town and city had at least two competing papers.

If the physical resonances between Tressell's time and today are marked, the comparison of attitudes is even more chilling. Thatcherism may be more sophisticated than the attitudes of Tressell's Robber Barons, Rushton, Didlum, Sweater and Grinder, but in some ways Thatcherism and Tebbitism is more aggressive. For the ragged trousered philanthropists, trade unionism was a prospect. Today it is receding as Rupert Murdoch and others cease to recognise unions in any part of their empires.

In our society, Tressell would find only too familiar the state of homelessness, with 126,000 households homeless last year, and 6000 sleeping rough on the streets. He would know the despair of women homeworkers, who *today* are earning £9.20 for a 49 hour week, pressing pins into plastic blocks; of 30p an hour for packing cards or for making Christmas crackers.

I hope that he would be as angry about what he would see today, as he was enraged by the way in which his characters accepted their lot. As Owen remarks, they are ragged trousered philanthropists because they are ready to slave their guts out for a pittance, to ensure the continued prosperity of their masters. They are positively eager to contribute to their own repression. It is their defeatism and lack of spirit which appals Owen as he battles to remove the scales from the eyes of his work mates, to reveal the working of the Great Money Trick, and to explain the need for socialism.

The Britain which re-elected Mrs Thatcher, for *her* Great Economic Miracle *twice* in spite of a record unemployment, a record collapse of manufacturing industry and record bankruptcies would surely make Owen, and Tressell, despair.

Of course it is true that in a material sense we have travelled a long way since the early years of the century. Washing machines and videos, cars and foreign holidays bear witness to that. But we're little nearer a fair or a just society, let alone the Golden Dawn of Socialism for which Owen longed with such passion.

The enduring strength of **The Ragged Trousered Philanthropists**, whether as a play or a novel, is that it reminds us, both of what we are fighting for and also that the battle is far from won. If Stephen Lowe's adaptation makes you open your eyes, not just to look again at the lives of Owen and the ragged trousered philanthropists, but to reconsider the world around us today, then it will have succeeded triumphantly. With that, Robert Tressell would be more than satisfied.

Mark Fisher, 1991
(*Shadow Minister for Arts and Media*)

Background

Robert Tressell, a pseudonym for Noonan, was born in Dublin in 1871 of a middle-class family. In his late teens he left for South Africa, where he worked as a signwriter and housepainter. Returning to England at the turn of the century, with his young daughter, Kathleen, he made what living he could by his trade in Hastings. Although housepainters were severely hit by the economic depression, it was a time of great activity and heated discussion within the British socialist tradition. The 1906 election was the first where the majority of the movement and the unions backed the emerging Labour party in its reformist, Parliamentary direction. Tressell was a member of the more Marxist Socialist Democratic Federation, which argued against that philosophy for some time. Decisions were made then which have affected all our lives.

He died in 1911, killed by tuberculosis, and was buried in an unmarked pauper's grave. In a savagely abridged version his book came out on the eve of war, in August 1914, the full text not being rediscovered and published until 1956, thanks largely to the single-minded dedication of his biographer, F.C. Ball. Against all the odds, the book has attained the status of the first major novel on the British working classes, and has become a socialist classic.

'The carpenter eats bread and meat
The bricklayer bread and cheese
But pity the poor painter
When the leaves fall off the trees.'

In 1906, *skilled* painters could earn £1.5s. in a good week, but they suffered from seasonal lay-offs and were not compensated for bad weather or daylight working restrictions.

Average cost of living for couple (no children)

Rent	7s	6d.
Food (potatoes/cheese)	6s	10d.
Meat (1 small leg of mutton)	2s	7d.
Coal, paraffin etc.	1s	3d.
Payment of essential furnishings	2s	0d.
£1.	0s	2d.

This excludes clothing, tools, travel, entertainment. In a bad week, when he is unemployed ('walking about') he receives nothing.

The Ragged Trousered Philanthropists was first performed by the Joint Stock Theatre Company in Plymouth on 14 September 1978, in a production which subsequently toured the country.

The play was revived at the Half Moon Theatre, London, on 13th July 1983, with the following cast:

Bob Crass, *site foreman – 7½p man*
Reverend Belcher, *holy man and Brigand* } Trevor Cooper

Frank Owen, *painter/signwriter – 7d. man*
Didlum, *food supplier and Brigand* } David Fielder

Sawkins, *labourer – 5d. man*
Mayor Sweater, *factory owner and Brigand* } Bob Goody

Bert White, *apprentice – no wages*
Elsie, *a waitress*
Mrs Sweater } Josie Lawrence

Joe Philpott, *painter – 7d. man*
Rushton, *owner of firm and Brigand* } Ken Morley

Will Easton, *painter – cut-rate worker*
Linden, *painter – 7d. man*
Grinder, *newspaper owner and Brigand* } Bill Thomas

Harlow, *painter – 7d. man*
Lettum, *landlord and Brigand* } Stephen Tiller

All the cast, except Trevor Cooper and David Fielder, play **Hunter**, the works foreman who earns 2½% of all profits.

Directed by John Adams   *General Manager* Graham Cowley
Designed by Mick Bearwish   *Production Manager* Neil Cooper
Lighting by Meg Smith   *Stage Managers* David Cooper, Meg Smith

Production Note
The men work continuously on the house, around, behind, between, above and in front of the audience. The central acting area is the 'kitchen'. Offices etc., are simply indicated with ladders, trestles, benches etc.

Almost all the actors' 'transformations', i.e. into Brigands, are played in sight of the audience. **Hunter's** hat and coat are visible on a dressmaker's dummy.

The Ragged Trousered Philanthropists was revived by the Birmingham Rep. in a touring production in February 1991, with the following cast:

Bob Crass, *site foreman – 7½p man*
Reverend Belcher, *holy man and Brigand* } Bob Hewis

Frank Owen, *painter/signwriter – 7d. man*
Didlum, *food supplier and Brigand* } Robert McIntosh

Sawkins, *labourer – 5d. man*
Mayor Sweater, *factory owner and Brigand* } Michael Gunn

Bert White, *apprentice – no wages*
Elsie, *a waitress*
Mrs Sweater } Helen Fitzgerald

Joe Philpott, *painter – 7d. man*
Rushton, *owner of firm and Brigand* } Peter Banks

Will Newman*, *painter – cut-rate worker*
Linden, *painter – 7d. man*
Grinder, *newspaper owner and Brigand* } Ian Blower

Harlow, *painter – 7d. man*
Lettum, *landlord and Brigand* } Tom Watt

All the cast, except Bob Hewis and Robert McIntosh, play **Hunter**, the works foreman who earns 2½% of all profits.
*Easton was renamed **Newman** for this production.

Directed by John Adams
Designed by Mick Bearwish
Lighting by Tim Mitchell
Decorating Technique by Bernard Faulkner

Company Manager Sally Isern
Production Manager Neil Cooper
Stage Managers Karen Gow, Peter Malvern, Rosie Gilbert, Charlotte Placquet

ACT ONE

THE START ON "THE CAVE"

(It is dark. The men wheel in a cart, overloaded with ladders, trestles, paints, etc. up to the house. CRASS unlocks the door and leads the men in.)

CRASS: Dump your gear in there. Bert, get them candles lit.
(The men put jackets, tool and food boxes in the scullery)

CRASS: Frank, you're on the upstairs front. Harlow, upstairs back. Bert, get the paint in. Linden, on the hallway. Sawkins, get the cart unloaded, and then clear out them drains.
*(The men set to work, by candlelight. CRASS sets up his paint table. The men cry out for Bert — 'Water' etc. — and begin washing the walls down, stripping paper, etc.
PHILPOTT walks to the dummy — puts on HUNTER'S coat and bowler hat.)*

HUNTER EMPLOYS A MAN AT CUT-RATE
(Hunter, the works foreman, stands over a coffin).

HUNTER: In the midst of life we is in death. Wood. Coffin, Plate, Etcetra. Eight shillings. Three pence. Men. Two men. Four hours. Seven pence a hour. Four shillings. Eight pence. Too much. Where's my two per cent profit go, at seven pence? Gobbled up by the men. Got to cut that. What profit? What profiteth?
(He trims the edges off the coffin with a saw. Easton, a young worker, waits, cap in hand).

EASTON: *(eventually)* Any hope, Mr Hunter, sir?

HUNTER: Full up. *(continues sawing)*

EASTON: Things been a bit rough, sir. Walking about fair bit, and now the missis's a young un on the way. Couple of days. Day even. I'd be ever so grateful.

HUNTER: Like t'elp. Doin' up Mayor Sweater's 'ouse. The Cave. Gi' you something. 'Elp out. You knows the going rate?

EASTON: Yes, sir.

HUNTER: Six and an' alf.

(Silence)

HUNTER: I'll tell Crass. Make a kit up for you. Start first thing. Seven. Seven o'clock. Sharp.

(Silence)

HUNTER: Take it or leave it. Free world.
EASTON: Thank you, sir.

(Easton exits)

HUNTER: *(begins sawing)* Cometh up and is cut down like a flower. Cost. Twelve shillings. Eleven pence. Cost to client. Three times. One pound. Eighteen shillings. Nine pence. Profit One pound five shillings ten pence. Two and a half per cent.

(Philpott places Hunter's cap and coat on the dummy)

BREAKFAST
(Crass checks his watch)

CRASS: BERT!
(Bert carries a large pail of tea)

CRASS: Rouse yourself, sonny. Draggin' your feet like you was at your mam's funeral. Want to 'ear the patter of your little feet when

I calls you. Kids run. That's why we took you on. Set it down there. Don't stand lookin' at it.
(Crass blows a whistle. The men stop working, and move to the 'kitchen' area).

CRASS: And make sure they've paints to start after breakfast.
(Crass helps himself to a cup of tea. Bert places two cooked bloaters on the table)

CRASS: Who's the big bloater for?

BERT: Mr Linden.
(Crass helps himself to the larger of the two. He sits down, takes out a paper, and begins to read. Harlow and Philpott enter).

HARLOW: How's it wi' yours?

PHILP: Covered with slime. Feel like a monkey climbing up a greased pole.

CRASS: Long as the paint sticks.

(Harlow and Philpott exchange glances. Owen enters)

PHILP: Tea's hot.

HARLOW: If nothin' else. Bloody Freezin' up there. Why we can't wear our top coats —

CRASS: You can. Just means you'll be walking about soon as Hunter spots you.
(Linden enters, and stares at the remaining bloater).

LINDEN: This in't mine. Mine 'ad its tail cut off. Eh, where the 'ell's mine?

BERT: I just put 'em both there.
(Linden tracks down the bloater to Crass).

CRASS: Sorry, is this yours Jack? Both looked the same to me.

LINDEN: Mine 'ad its tail cut off.

CRASS: You can 'ave it back. I've only took a couple of bites.

LINDEN: S'all right Bob.

CRASS: Allers look forward to a nice bloater.

LINDEN: So do I.

(Sawkins enters. He is covered in muck).

SAWKINS: Where am I goin' to sit?

PHILP: Not near me.

CRASS: You been rollin' in it, 'ave you?

SAWKINS: Them bloody drains been blocked for years. Fuck'n' job that is.

PHILP: Bert'll bring your breakfast outside.

SAWKINS: Don't come it.

PHILP: Pullin' your leg.

CRASS: Puttin' me off me bloater.

SAWKINS: Fuckin' job.

CRASS: Should 'ave done your time shun't you? Woun't 'ave to take the shit. Done your time like the rest of us.

SAWKINS: Won't open to me, was it?

HARLOW: Won't open to any of us, but we still done it.

SAWKINS: Shift off, Bert.

BERT: Sorry, Mr Sawkins.

SAWKINS: Sittin' on the best seat. Kids get it better than I do. Get our tea, will you?

BERT: All right.
(he does so)

(Sawkins picks up the 'penny 'orrible' that Bert was reading. He mouths the words, reading with considerable difficulty)

OWEN: You read that book I lent you?

BERT: Nearly. Din't bring it in 'cos it'd only get dirty.

PHILP: You down the Cricketers last night?

CRASS: Got to keep me seat, an't I? Thought you might be in, to buy me one. Seein' as how well I looks after you.

PHILP: Fell off the slate there, Bob. 'Til I can gi' 'em someat come Saturday.

LINDEN: Join the Sally Army.

PHILP: Not while the Dog and Bear's still open.

CRASS: Tinker's pub is that.

PHILP: Not so bad.

CRASS: Shit house. 'E pisses in the beer, Just to gi' it a bit of 'ead.

HARLOW: Come on.

CRASS: God strike me dead.

PHILP: You're puttin' our Frank off his breakfast.

CRASS: Our artist. *(winks at Philpott)* Planning a nice bit of fancy work on that room, are you, Frank?

OWEN: Nice mural, you know. Country scene.

CRASS: Wount surprise me. Time it's takin' you to wash down. Doin' a Muriel. That's her name, innit?

PHILP: Who?

CRASS: Down the Dog.

PHILP: Maud.

CRASS: Doin' a Maud. Fancy that.

PHILP: Face like the arse of a carthorse.

CRASS: Don't look at the mantlepiece when you's pokin' the fire.

HARLOW: Could do wi' some fires here. Dry these walls out.

SAWKINS: *(while reading)* DORM-I-TORY.
(he looks up. The men laugh. He throws the paper at Bert).

SAWKINS: Load of shit that is. Wastin' your money on that.

BERT: I don't buy them.

PHILP: Oh aye?

BERT: I find them.

PHILP: Likely tale.

BERT: I find them back of the big houses.

LINDEN: Them's not yours. You'll end up in trouble, will you.

CRASS: He'll end up in trouble wi' me if he don't start movin' 'imself a bit.
(Bert leaves)

SAWKINS: Anything for the big race?

PHILP: Anybody's. Never bet over the sticks you know. Mug's game.

SAWKINS: Neither do I.

CRASS: (reading from his paper).

3

Bleedin' foreigners. Take the bread right out your bleedin' mouth. Says here. they's swampin' the shops wi'all their foreign junk.

HARLOW: They're over here an' all. Selling their onions.

SAWKINS: Italians are the worse. You can't go in a really posh restaurant wi'out one of them greasy buggers servin' you.

LINDEN: No wonder there's no work for our lads.

PHILP: I seen a Italian organ grinder down Old Street, with a monkey collectin' wi' a tin can.
(Owen laughs)

SAWKINS: What's the big joke?

OWEN: You should send the monkey back. Give the job to one of our English monkeys.

CRASS: Funny is it? Our lads starvin'?

LINDEN: I don't see anything to laugh at.

OWEN: I'm not laughing. I'm wi' you. I mean it's as plain as the nose on your face God made big mistake making all these foreigners.

LINDEN: Right.

OWEN: We should send him a letter, telling him to shut down production.

HARLOW: 'Ave to put your a'porth in, don't you?

CRASS: Course he does. 'As to think different, don't he? Woun't do to think like the rest of us.

LINDEN: Just don't go starting on about politics again. Only ends in a bloody row and does nobody any good.

PHILP: Hear, hear.

SAWKINS: I never bothers me 'ead about politics.

OWEN: Doesn't stop you votin' though, does it?

SAWKINS: I pays me rates and taxes. I've as much right to vote as the next man.

PHILP: What's the sense? It don't make no difference who you votes for.

CRASS: Long as they're Tory.

PHILP: Fact is, they're all working the 'orricle for their own ends. Talk 'til you're black in the face, won't change that. It's no use worrying about it. Just make the best of it.

HARLOW: Make the best of a bad job.

PHILP: That's what I'm sayin'.

OWEN: Do you say that when you're walking about?

SAWKINS: What's the point talkin' about walkin' about? We're in work now.

LINDEN: Don't tempt fate, that's what I always say.

HARLOW: Come on, Frank, even you've got to admit it. There's too many blokes after too few jobs, and 'aving foreigners in, don't make it no better. Bound to be poverty wi' all that, in't there?

OWEN: No bound about it.

CRASS: Hoverpopulation. That's what it's called.

LINDEN: Young 'uns. Want to get married too quick.

OWEN: Tell Harlow and his four kids.

4

LINDEN: Ah well, that's different.

OWEN: It's got nothing to do with it, anyway. There's still thousands of acres of uncultivated land in England, and there's *(he starts coughing)*.

CRASS: Well, that's shut him up, at any rate.

PHILP: Slap your back.
(Owen shakes his head)

CRASS: Knock some sense into him.

PHILP: Getting worse innit?

LINDEN: You ask me, it's this eddication. Too much of it nowdays. What's the good of it for the likes of us?

CRASS: No good is it? Just puts daft ideas in folks 'eads, and makes 'em too lazy for work. Most of these buggers who go about pleadin' poverty never done a decent days' work in their lives.

SAWKINS: That's right, is that

LINDEN: And what about drink?

PHILP: Mine's a pint.

OWEN: *(recovering)* What you goin' on about drink and laziness for? They're all red herrings.

PHILP: Wish they were.

OWEN: If all the drunks and skivers went back to work tomorrow it wouldn't help all us who are working. It would only make us poorer with lower wages, and increased unemployment.

LINDEN: Eh up, he's back.

OWEN: You must see the reason we're poor has nothing to do with any of these things.

CRASS: I'll tell you what it is, mate. I don't need you to tell me. I'll tell you.

SAWKINS: What?

CRASS: It's these bleedin' machines they keep inventing. Doin' blokes out of work left right and centre. I've heard tell some bastard has even bought out a paintin' machine.

LINDEN: No?

SAWKINS: How does that work then?

OWEN: Machines may cause unemployment, but they're not the cause of poverty.

HARLOW: Same difference.

OWEN: Not at all. Poverty means lacking the necessaries of life. It's nothing to do with working or not. We work, and we still lack them. We don't 'ave decent food, 'ouses that are fit to live in wi'out fear of disease, don't have decent clothes. We all dread when it rains, in case our boots let in water and we end up laid up. Now if you think that machines, which can make all these things in large numbers, are the cause of our being short of them, there must be something wrong with your minds.

CRASS: We knows we's all fools bar you. When they gi's out sense, they gi's you such a 'ell of a lot there won't none left for the likes of us.

SAWKINS: I don't know about that.

OWEN: You think that if there were no machines, if we had plenty of WORK — if we slaved away fourteen fifteen hours a day, we wouldn't still find ourselves living in poverty? You're fooling yourselves. Don't attack the machines. They could solve our needs.

CRASS: What is it then, smart-arse?

OWEN: It's like everything else. It's who owns the machines. Who takes what they produce. They are owned, and worked solely for the benefit of, a small group of men, the Capitalists —

LINDEN: I've been waiting for them.

CRASS: An' we all?

OWEN: You fight yourselves when you fight machines. They only do the work, and get no benefit from it. Just the same as us. We're their machines now, and when we get old or no more use to them, they replace us with younger, more profitable machines, and kick us out to rust or starve to death.

CRASS: Come on, lads, Time to get back.

LINDEN: Be a pleasure.

OWEN: We'd be better off if we were slaves. The owners in their own interest would see to it that we always had enough food and—

LINDEN: 'Ere. You speak for yourself, mate. I can tell you I don't put myself down as no slave.

CRASS: Nor me neither. Let them call theirselves slaves as want to.

(Bert struggles through the door, making a noise)

CRASS: Christ; HUNTER!

(The men freeze, petrified. When they see Bert, they groan, and jeer).

CRASS: BERT!

LINDEN: What you trying to do — give us 'eart-attack?

CRASS: You ever do that again, and you'll not sit down for a week.

BERT: What?

CRASS: You know what.
(the men go back to work).

HUNTER'S VISIT
(The house is now silent except for the sound of work).
(Philpott is "stopping". Old Linden mumbles away to himself, while carefully pumicestoning the front door frame).

LINDEN: Calls themselves painters. Bloody teardrops all over the shop. Woun't have lasted five minutes. No feel for wood. Bit of respect woun't do 'em no harm. Respect the wood, and it'll respect you. Goes all through the grain. Go wi' the grain. All through your life. Respect the bosses and they respects you.

(He looks up to find Hunter,[Sawkins] looming over him. He sandpapers, frantically. Hunter stands silent).
(Hunter creeps through the house, silently, unnoticed.)
(Hunter stands watching Harlow, who at first does not realise it. When he does, he drops his brush, picks it up and begins to paint even faster, slobbering the paint everywhere including over himself; Hunter stands, silent. He leaves the room. Philpott, who has been working on top of a ladder, decides to risk a quick smoke. He jams the door with his ladder, and opens a window. He perches on his ladder, and starts up his pipe.)

PHILPOTT: This is where we get a bit of our own back.

(Hunter stands watching Owen, paint. Eventually, Owen slowly turns until they are staring at each other. Hunter finally turns away. Owen turns back. He is visibly shaking.)
(Hunter tries Philpott's door. Philpott buries his pipe into his pocket, opens the door. Hunter enters. He sniffs the air.

6

Philpott closes the door then resumes work).

HUNTER: *(eventually)* Don't care for men workin' with the door shut. Allers gi' me the idear they's havin a mike. Can do what you're doin' just as well with the door open.

PHILPOTT: *(quietly)* All the same to me. *(He opens the door. Hunter watches him working)*

HUNTER: Don't want no hartwork on that there cornice. Ain't no hangels goin' to fly up there to take a gander. *(He leaves the room and discovers Crass painting the scullery).*

HUNTER: Crass! Paint! *(Crass follows Hunter to the kitchen, where Hunter waters down the paint).*

CRASS: Mr Hunter, sir.

HUNTER: Burning. Profits. Pennies.

CRASS: Yes, sir.

HUNTER: Look after the pennies, Crass

CRASS: And the pounds'll look —

HUNTER: What?

CRASS: Nothing sir.

HUNTER: *(trying the diluted paint on the wall)* New man. Easton. Seven o'clock. *(Hands him the paint).*

CRASS: Yes sir.

HUNTER: Too many seven penny men. Can't run to it. I sees halterations, Crass.
(Silence)
HUNTER: You with me?

CRASS: Yes sir.

HUNTER: Well?

CRASS: That Owen, sir. He's awkward.

HUNTER: Awkward?

CRASS: Stirrer, sir. Wi' his far-fetched idears.

HUNTER: Owen. Sign writers. Hartists. What do we want wi' hartists?

CRASS: What indeed, sir. And then there's them old men, sir. It's them what's holdin' us back. Turn your back, and they's sanding down. Allers tryin' to do it proper. Makes your heart bleed.

HUNTER: Old men.
(Hunter nods. Crass returns to work. Hunter crosses to Linden).

HUNTER: How much longer is you thinkin' of messin' about on them doors? Why don't you put them under colour? You think it pays you playing there hour after hour? Been noticing your style. You can't play the fool wi' me. If you can't do it more quickly then clear out. We can do wi'out yor sort even when we're busy.

LINDEN: *(almost inarticulate)* I must clean the work down, sir. 'For I go on with the painting.

HUNTER: I ain't talkin' about what you's doing, but the time it takes you to do it. And I don't want no back answers or arguments about it. You must move yourself a bit quicker or leave it alone all together.
(Hunter leaves. The men work, unsure if Hunter has gone. Philpott throws a ball of paper across the hall to attract Owen's attention. He mimes "Has he gone?" Owen shrugs, not knowing, and returns to work. Philpott creeps gingerly down stairs. He whispers to Crass, who kicks Bert out from under the table, to go see. Bert leaves the house).
CRASS: *(whispering)* Who the bleedin' hell does he think he is?
PHILP: God alone knows. *(loudly)* Mix us up some.

7

CRASS: Never does to take the shit of 'em. If they don't like me work. Fair enough. Pay me off. Pack me kit and away, Rather walk about than be kicked like a dog.

PHILP: You and me both.
(Bert runs in)

BERT: He's gone.

CRASS: Thank God for that.
(Bert runs around to let the men know. Philpott goes to Linden)

PHILP: You all right?

LINDEN: Yes.

PHILPOTT: 'Ere 'Ave a smoke.

LINDEN: Don't know as I should.

PHILP: Can't let the bastards see they're beatin' you.

LINDEN: Won't stop me workin', will it?

PHILP: Work all the better. He won't be back now.

LINDEN: Could do wi' it, ta.

(He fills his pipe)
(Owen crosses to the kitchen for more paint)

CRASS: Thinks he's bleedin' God. That's the trouble. But he in't no better than us. He was a journeyman just the same as us. Any of us could do his job. Anyone prepared to graft and do some brain work.

OWEN: Anybody who wants his job.

(Philpott takes his tobacco and returns for his paint. Linden lights the pipe).

CRASS: Don't gi' me that. We all want to better ourselves.

OWEN: You call Hunter bettering yourself?

PHILP: Bit of the old stirring, eh, Frank?

CRASS: I'm the stirrer round here, I mixes the paint. You after my job?

OWEN: Not in a million years.

CRASS: Ye', well they all say that. Then as soon as your back's turned, they're up and on wi' your coat.

PHILP: Only human nature that. Every man for himself.

OWEN: Whats' human nature got to do wi' it? Human nature is for human beings. We don't know anything about them. All we know is dog eats dog, and that —

CRASS: Put a cork in it, will you?

(Linden opens the door to discover Hunter)

HUNTER: Right!

(Owen and Philpott dart back to their rooms)

HUNTER: I don't pay you for smoking. Make out your time sheet, take it to the office and get your money. I've had enough of the likes of you.

(Hunter tours the house, and exits, as Linden packs his stuff away. The men stop and watch Linden, before commencing work. Linden closes the door behind him. Harlow crosses to Owen)

HARLOW: *(Whispering)* Any stopping, Frank?

OWEN: Help yourself.

HARLOW: I'll swing for that bastard, that I will. How does a misery like that get in charge of men?

OWEN: He gets the job 'cos he's good at it.

8

HARLOW: Good at it? Good at knocking the shit out of old men?

OWEN: Good at knocking the shit out of all of us.

HARLOW: You speak for yourself, mate.

OWEN: Listen, it's not the men you should be railing against. It's the rotten system that makes them the men they are.

HARLOW: Oh, ye'. Well, we've heard your lectures, but nobody's going to tell me you 'ave to be a bastard like that. *(He walks back to his room)*

THE MOORISH ROOM

(Bert runs into the house. He careers around until he locates Owen. Philpott and Crass follow on to see what is happening. Bert is breathless. Easton follows him in, standing with his tool bag, waiting for orders.)

OWEN: Take it easy, kid. Or you'll end up like me.

CRASS: What's the game?

OWEN: Seen a ghost, have you?

CRASS: Spit it out.

BERT: He says —

CRASS: Who says?

OWEN: Get your breath.

BERT: Mr Hunter —

OWEN: Hunter? What does he want?

BERT: Got to . . . Go to . . . The shop. Straight off. Told me. Run. All the way.

OWEN: What for?
BERT: Report to Rushton.

(Silence)

CRASS: What you been up to then?

OWEN: You heard anything, Bob?

CRASS: Talk of a slaughter.

OWEN: Not first thing on a Monday. They woun't lay a man off on a Monday.

CRASS: Who's to say what they'll do?

PHILPOTT: You'd better get down there, Frank.

OWEN: Yes.

PHILPOTT: Listen, if he lays you off, you charge 'til six. You've come in.

CRASS: Ye'. You try that.

(Owen hands his tools to Bert, and leaves)
(Crass notices Easton)

CRASS: You Easton?

EASTON: Will Easton, ye!

CRASS: Dump your clobber through there.

EASTON: Right.

(As he changes —)

CRASS: What you like wi' wood?

EASTON: I know me way round a saw.

CRASS: Well, there's some skirting to be done. Patchwork. Top of the stairway.

EASTON: What was that all about then?

CRASS: Your guess. Mind you, Frank's allers shooting his mouth off about politics. Socialist claptrap. You know the sort of thing.

9

EASTON: Ye'.

CRASS: Bosses bound to 'ear about it, aren't they? They don't miss much.

EASTON: No.

CRASS: Biting the 'and that feeds you. That's.no way, is it?

EASTON: It certainly isn't.

(He begins work, replacing the skirting on the outside of Philpott's room).

(Rushton sits at his desk. Owen stands waiting).

RUSHTON: Fancy yourself as a bit of a Hartist, don't you?

OWEN: How do you mean?

RUSHTON: Mayor Sweater taken a fancy to have his drawing-room done up like a room he saw in Paris. Walls and ceiling not papered, but painted; sort of panelled out, and decorated with stencils and handpainting. 'Ere's a photo. Sort of Japanese style.

OWEN: Moorish.

RUSHTON: First he thought of getting a London firm up but he gave that up on account of the expense. But if you can do it, and it don't cost too much, I might be able to talk him into it. Course, if it's too dear, he'll just have a frieze put up, and 'ave it papered in the normal fashion. Question is, are you up to it?

OWEN: Yes. Yes, I think I am.

RUSHTON: Woun't want you to start, and not be able to deliver. Are you then, or aren't you?

OWEN: Best thing is if I make a water-colour sketch — a design — and see if you think it's good enough —

RUSHTON: Oh ye'. I let you spend time over drawings, then the Mayor don't like it, and I'm out of pocket, aren't I?

OWEN: I mean, I'll do them at home — in my own time.

RUSHTON: All right, Bring 'em in tomorrow.

OWEN: I can't do that. It'll take some thinking about.

RUSHTON: When then? Wednesday first thing? *(Owen hesitates)* We can't afford to keep him waiting too long, or he may give up the idea altogether.

OWEN: If I work all night, I could guarantee something Thursday.

RUSHTON: All right. But don't pile it on too thick, or we'll have to charge so much he won't have it done at all. *(he continues with his work).*

OWEN: Can I take the photo?

RUSHTON: Hm.

(Owen takes the photo and leaves)

(Owen is working on his drawings)

OWEN: Pick out the window. Good window. Let's the light in. Light. Sky beyond. A pattern across the walls and ceiling. A Moroccan. Same basic pattern, simple pattern but twisting and turning through a cycle. Developing as it goes. Flowing round and round the walls. Like sitting in a room full of music. Walls picking up, embroidering, replaying the same basic theme. A theme in gold. Gold leaf not gold paint. Don't spoil it for a a'porth of tar. Gold leaf on a clean white base. I could do someat wi' that. Someat wonderful.

(Easton is nailing the skirting outside Philpott's room' Sweater enters the house)

10

EASTON: Bit of dry rot down here.

PHILPOTT: I sometimes feel I've a bit of dry rot meself.

EASTON: Here, Mayor Sweater's paying us a visit.

PHILPOTT: I thinks we ought to seize this tuneropperty to touch him for a small allowance.

EASTON: You'll get no change out of him, mate. Red hot teetotaller is him. Shining Light Chapel.

PHILPOTT: How's he to know we buy beer wi' it? We might have tea, or ginger ale, or lime juice and glycerine for all he knows. *(He crosses to Moorish Room)*. Morning, sir. Harlow.

HARLOW: Hallo.

PHILPOTT: Give us a hand here, will you? *(They start to erect trestles)*

HARLOW: Morning, sir.

PHILPOTT: How is things up your end?

HARLOW: All right, you know.

PHILPOTT: Pretty dry job, isn't it?

HARLOW: Yes, it is. Rather.

PHILPOTT: Think this would be a good time to take up the collection, do you?

HARLOW: Ye' it woun't be a bad idear.

PHILPOTT: Well, I'll just put my cap on the stairs. You never knows your luck. Some kind Christian might drop a coin in it. Things are getting serious on this floor, you know. My mate's fainted once already.

(He waits for some reaction. Gets none)

PHILPOTT: I allers reckon a man can work all the better after 'e's had a drink; you can seem to get over more of it, like.

HARLOW: That's true enough. I've often noticed it myself.

(Sweater reaches into his pocket. He takes out a handkerchief, blows his nose and steps over the cap)

HARLOW: *(whispering)* I'm afraid it's a frost, mate.

PHILPOTT: *(picking up cap)* I knowed a case once where a chap died — of thirst — on a job like this, and at the inquest the doctor said a pint would a' saved him.

EASTON: It must have been a terrible death.

PHILPOTT: Terrible. It was something chronic.

(Sweater walks out, unseeing)

OWEN: Just gi' me the chance of it, eh? I could do a good job. No slapping paint over rotten wood. Hearing the worms chewing away behind the paint. No papering over cracks. Burn the paint right back. Strip it down. Treat the walls. Stop the cracks. Dry it out. Clean base. Three coats of white. Clean canvas. No wood that crumbles to dust. No wall to powder. Real work. Just once. I'm due. It's my right. Gi' it to me.

(Owen waits. Rushton enters his office)

RUSHTON: Oh, yess, the sketches. There was no need to hang about, you know. You could have left 'em and gone on to your job. *(he glances carelessly over the designs)*.

OWEN: That's for the ceiling. I hadn't time to colour all of it. That's for the .arge wall. The same design would be

11

adapted for the other walls; and that's the door and the panels under the window.

RUSHTON: How long will it take?

OWEN: About three weeks – 150 hours. That's the decorative work only. The— it'll need three coats of white first.

RUSHTON: *(casually)* Well, we'll see.

(Owen stays on)

OWEN: And I'll need some help. A man occasionally, and the boy most of the time. Then there's gold leaf – say fifteen books.

RUSHTON: Gold leaf? Whats' wrong wi' gold paint?

OWEN: It won't do.

RUSHTON: Anything else?

OWEN: Few sheets of cartridge paper for stencils, and working drawings. The amount of paint necessary for decorative work is very small.

(Owen leaves)

RUSHTON: Excellent. Good enough for anywhere. If he can paint half so well on the walls, it'll stand all the looking at. Hunter!

(Hunter [Harlow] enters)

RUSHTON: Said it'd take him three weeks, but he was so keen to do the job he was underestimating. Say, four. 200 hours. What's the rate?

HUNTER: Hartistic work. Seven and a half.

RUSHTON: Plus a man half-time at seven.

HUNTER: £9 the two. Approximately.

RUSHTON: Fifteen books of gold.

HUNTER: One pound.

RUSHTON: Cartridge paper, colours – what?

HUNTER: Another pound at the outside.

RUSHTON: Boy's time.

HUNTER: First year apprentice. No wages.

RUSHTON: Three coats of white?

HUNTER: Three?

RUSHTON: Got to be done proper this one.

HUNTER: Three pounds five.

RUSHTON: All in all.

HUNTER: Less than fifteen pounds.

RUSHTON: Charge Sweater forty-five for that, eh? It'd cost him twice that to bring them in from London, which he's thinking of doing. I think we can say, go ahead on that.

(Rushton hands the drawings to Hunter. Hunter gives them to Owen. He and Bert begin work in the Moorish Room. Crass is mixing paint for Sawkins and Easton)

CRASS: Well, what do you mek of it, eh?

EASTON: Mek of what?

CRASS: Our little artist mate; you think he's goin' to pull it off, do you?

EASTON: Shun't like to say.

SAWKINS: Not a 'ope, has he?

CRASS: One thing to draw on a scrap of paper and colour it wi' a penny box of paints, quite another doin' it big up on a wall or ceiling, in't it?

SAWKINS: Too true, mate.

CRASS: You reckon them's 'is own designs?

EASTON: Hard to tell, innit?

CRASS: If you was to ask my opinion, I should be hinclined to say he copied 'em straight out of some book.

SAWKINS: No question.

CRASS: *(winking)* Be a crying shame if he was to make a shit of it, woun't it?

SAWKINS: Not 'arf.

(The two men take their paint, and, laughing, together, meet Philpott on the stairs)

PHILP: Come on, Let me in on the joke.

SAWKINS: Crass is losin' his rag over Owen doin' that there room.

PHILP: Bit of a take down for the bugger, innit, playing the second fiddle.

EASTON: He's praying he comes a cropper.

PHILP: Fat chance. Our Frank knows his way round his paints, and no mistake. He's got his head screwed on when it comes to paint.

SAWKINS: Well, he's off his onions when it comes to politics.

PHILP: Well, maybe.

EASTON: Always goes to far, don't he?

(Crass is attempting to creep up on them)

SAWKINS: Here!
(Crass appears)

CRASS: You'd better look alive, lads. If we don't get these ceilings done by evening, old Misery's sure to ramp.

SAWKINS: We'll soon get it sloshed on for you.

(They begin to work)

(Hunter watches Owen, who is working quietly, carefully on the arch)

HUNTER: Takin' its time, this job. Takin' its time.

OWEN: Mr Rushton said to do it proper.

HUNTER: And costing. Costing.

OWEN: I'll need to do some more working drawings.

HUNTER: What? Working drawings? What the hell are all these?

OWEN: The pattern changes as it works round the walls. I have to make full-sized drawings, with perforated outlines, to transfer the design.

HUNTER: Can't you just copy them on the wall, free-hand?

OWEN: No, that wouldn't do. It would take much longer that way.

HUNTER: Well, I s'pose you'll have to have it the way you said; but for goodness sake don't spend too much time on it, because we've took it very cheap. We only took it so you could 'ave a job, not that we expect to make a profit out of it.

OWEN: I shall have to cut some stencils, so I shall need more cartridge paper.

13

HUNTER: Good grief, man! *(Pause)* Here. I tell you what. Lots of odd rolls of wallpaper down the shop. Make do with them.

OWEN: They won't do.

(Hunter groans. Speechless, he leaves the room)

HUNTER: *(Shouting)* ROUSE YOURSELVES! You all seem to think this is a 'orspital. If you all don't make a better show of it, there's goin' to be some Halterations here. Plenty of blokes walking about, be glad of your job! There ain't the work to keep you all in comfort.

(He goes. The men work on desperately)

THE GREAT MONEY-TRICK
(Dinner break — the kitchen)

CRASS: Wot's become of the Professor then?

HARLOW: P'raps he's preparin' his sermon.

EASTON: We an't had no lectures from 'im lately, since he's been working on the droring-room.

SAWKINS: Damn good job. Gi's me the pip to hear 'im, the same thing over and over again.

HARLOW: 'E does upset himself about things, don't he?

SAWKINS: Well, what's the use the likes of us worryin' our 'eads about politics?

HARLOW: I don't see that. We've got votes, so we ought to take some interest but I don't see no sense in this 'ere Socialist wangle that Frank's always talking about.

CRASS: Nor does nobody else either.

EASTON: But 'e had a cuff the other day about money being no good at all. Goin' on about money being the main cause of poverty.

(Owen enters)

OWEN: So it is — the main cause of poverty.

HARLOW: Here we go again.

PHILP: Gentl'men. Professor Owen is goin' to give us 'is well known lecture, Money the Main Cause of Bein' Ard Up, proving as money an't no good to nobody. At the hend a collection will be took to encourage the lecturer.

OWEN: Let me eat me dinner.

PHILP: Come on, Frank.

CRASS: See, It's all very good saying these things. Provin' it is a different thing.

OWEN: Right. I'll show you the great Money Trick. Now for the purpose of this demonstration I shall need the help of members of the audience. May I borrow your knife, sir?

(He collects knives from Harlow, Philpott, Easton)

OWEN: Has anybody got any bread they can spare?

(He adds the bread he collects to his own)

OWEN: These pieces of bread represent the raw materials which exist naturally in and on the earth for the use of mankind; they were not made by any human being, but were created by the the Great Spirit for the benefit and sustenance of all, the same as were the air and the light and the sun.

HARLOW: Well, that's nice and clear.

PHILP: Clear as mud.

14

OWEN: Now. I am a Capitalist. And all these raw materials belong to me. Don't matter for now how I got hold of them, or whether I have any right to them. Fact is that all the raw materials are now the property of the Landlord and Capitalist class. That's me.

PHILP: Good enough.

OWEN: And you three. *(Harlow, Easton, Philpott)* are the Working Classes; you have nothing and while I've got all this raw material, they are no use to me — what I need are the things that are made out of these raw materials by Work; but I am too lazy to work myself, so I have invented the Great Money Trick to make you work for me. Now not only do I own all the raw materials, but these three knives stand for all the machinery, all the tools of production; factories, railways. And these three coins *(takes three halfpennies from his pocket)* stand for my Money Capital. Got it?

CRASS: We got it. Git on with it. *(Owen cuts on of the slices of bread into small square blocks)*

OWEN: These squares represent the things which are produced by labour, aided by machinery, from the raw materials. Let's say three of these blocks make a week's work; And let's say each of these ha'pennies is a sovereign. We'd be able to do the trick better if we had real sovereigns, but I forgot to bring any with me.

PHILP: I'd lend you some. But I left me purse on the grand pianner.

OWEN: Now you three say you are in need of work, and as I am a kind-hearted Capitalist I am going to invest all my money in industries, to give you PLENTY OF WORK. I'll pay you a pound a week, and for a week's work you must produce three of these square blocks. Then I give you a pound. I take what you produce, but you can do whatever you want with the pound. Fair enough? Set to then.

(The men cut the pieces into threes)

OWEN: Here's your pound. *(he gathers the pieces to himself)* Now these blocks represent the necessities of life. Food, Housing, Clothing, Everything. Now you can't live without them, so you've got to buy them off me. And my price for one of these is — one pound.

(The men buy and devour the bread)

OWEN: I'll have two 'cos I'm greedy. So I've got four pounds in produce, me three sovereigns back, what you got?

PHILP: Nothing. I just ate it.

OWEN: Want to work then, do you?

MEN: Ye' course we do.

OWEN: Off we go, then.

(They repeat this several times, until a pile of wealth has accumulated for the Capitalist).
(Owen suddenly grabs back the knives from the men)

MEN: Here, what's going on?

OWEN: Bad news, chaps. Owing to Over Production all my warehouses are glutted with the necessaries of life. So I've decided to close down the works.

PHILP: What the bloody 'ell are we to do then?

OWEN: That's not my business. I've paid your wages, fair and square, given you PLENTY OF WORK for a long time. No more work at present. Come round in a couple of months.

HARLOW: But what about the necessaries of life? We've got to eat someat, an't we?

OWEN: Course you have. And I shall be very pleased to sell you some.

EASTON: But we ain't got no bleedin' money.

OWEN: Well, you don't expect me to gi' you my stuff for nothing. You din't work for me for nothing. I paid you. You should have saved something. Should have been thrifty, like me!

PHILP: Here, if you don't gi' us something, what's to stop us takin' it.

OWEN: I appeal to your sense of decency. Fair play.

PHILP: That don't wash wi' us, mate. We're hungry.

OWEN: If you are not more polite, I'll have to get my friends the police down here, and they may be forced to bash your faces in, so as to protect an honest man from villains.

HARLOW: Well, that about takes the biskit.

EASTON: What are we going to do?

PHILP: We'll 'ave to 'ave an unemployed procession.

(They make a procession).

MEN: *(sing)*
We got no work to do
We got no work to do.
We've been working too damned hard.
We've got no work to do.

(The crowd jeer at them, and try to spit in their hats)

PHILP: We won't get nothing out of this lot. Let's try the old religious dodge, that always makes them part up.

HARLOW: Trim your feeble lamp . . . .

(The others join in the song. At the end the kind Capitalist drops a coin in)

PHILP: A sovereign. Bless you, sir.

OWEN: What are you goin' to do wi' it, my good man?

PHILP: Buy food.

OWEN: There you are. *(He takes the coin back)*

(The unemployed sing For He's A Jolly Good Fellow).

HARLOW: Here, Mr Kind Capitalist, would you allow us to elect you to Parliament?
(BLACKOUT)

THE THREATENED SLAUGHTER

(Owen and Bert work on the Moorish room. Easton and Harlow are painting the last coat of paint on the woodwork. Crass and Philpott work quietly in different parts of the house. All their tasks are silent. Occasionally they stop and listen out. When they speak they whisper)

HARLOW: What time is it?

EASTON: Dunno.

HARLOW: If he in't here by twelve, we'll be allright for another week.

EASTON: He won't lay us wi' the outing this afternoon will he?

HARLOW: You're kidding. He'd love to put a stop to our Beano.

EASTON: But there must be another week's work here. All the outside for the final coat.

HARLOW: Or a couple of weeks for two men. You don't know what Crass 'as been planning behind our backs.

(Owen is teaching Bert to transfer gold leaf from book to wall)

OWEN: Just flick your brush lightly 'cross your cheek: Pick up a bit of oil, you see. Now then, it should lift the edge of the gold leaf. That's it. Now gently breathe on it, and it'll lift off. Let the air take it. *(He coughs)* 'Scuse me. Just showing you what you shouldn't do. Now, blow it, guide it with the brush onto the wall. You've got it. Now let me show you how to whisper it flat. You just quietly chat the creases out of it. Come on, you lovely. There we go.

BERT: It in't like work at all, in't this.

OWEN: It is work.

(Philpott whispers to Crass)

PHILP: Any news?

CRASS: Nothing.

PHILP: What time is it?

CRASS: Ten to.

PHILP: Not come will he?

CRASS: Woun't take bets.

PHILP: No.

(Bert and Owen)

BERT: He'll not lay you off today.

OWEN: Still a week's work here. Then who knows?

BERT: Might be another job like this.

OWEN: They don't grow on trees, you know.

HARLOW: This is a bloody life innit? Workin' our guts out like slaves for them, and as soon as they've done with you, you're chucked out like a dirty rag.

EASTON: Keep it down, eh? Seen the steps?

HARLOW: Crass's got 'em. Ask him what the bleedin' time is?

(Easton crosses to Crass).

EASTON: Borrow your steps?

CRASS: Yes.

EASTON: What time is it?

CRASS: Nearly five to.

EASTON: He won't come now, will he?

CRASS: What you worried about? YOU'LL be the last to go.

EASTON: How do you mean?

CRASS: Come on. Don't play it wi' me. I'm the coddy. Not much gets by me. Not even a a'penny.

EASTON: It was for the kid's sake. Not mine.

CRASS: No skin off my nose. Just keep me smiling, you'll be alright. *(He hands him the paint)*

CRASS: Don't worry, Your secret's safe with me. Safe as houses.

(Easton walks back to door)

EASTON: HUNTER!

(By the time Hunter [Bert] enters, the men are painting furiously. When Hunter leaves the men quietly gather)

HARLOW: Did he say anything to you?

CRASS: Not a dicky.

HARLOW: God.

PHILIP: Another week, eh?

EASTON: Maybe he's got another job on then, eh? Soon as this is done.

HARLOW: A big job eh? Maybe a hotel, or someat.

SAWKINS: Or a big posh restaurant.

CRASS: Maybe.

PHILP: The dinner would 'ave been like the last Supper, if he'd knifed us.

HARLOW: I'd have killed the bugger 'aving paid in all year for it.

CRASS: Come on, lads. 'Nother half hour, and then home and get yourselves spruced up in your Sunday best. Let's get this place cleared up a bit. We'll be outside next week.

(They quietly go back to work, then start clearing the room)

HARLOW: *(Singing)*
Work for the night is coming
Work in the morning hours
Work for the night is coming
Work mid springing flowers
(the men join in)
Work while the dew is sparkling
Work in the noon day sun
Work for the night is coming
When man's work is done!

PHILP: *(imitating whine of street singer)*
Oh, where is my wandering boy tonight?
The boy of my tenderest care
The boy that was once my joy and light,
the child of my love and prayer?

Oh, where is my boy tonight?
Oh, where is my boy tonight?
My heart o'er flows,
for I love him, he knows,
Oh where is my boy tonight?

(This is greeted by catcalls, jeers etc.)

(Harlow takes a coin out of his pocket, and drops it on the floor).

PHILP: Thank you, kind lady.

(This sets off a chain among the men, flipping coins, everyone crying God Bless you sir, Thank you sir, etc.. From this everyone strikes up different songs, finally settling on a rousing chorus of Many a Time).

For we'd both been there before many a time, many a time
We'd both been there before many a time
Where many a gallon of beer had gone to colour his nose and mine
and we'd both been there before many a time, many a time.

CRASS: Ere! For crying out loud make less racket! Suppose old Misery was to come back?

HARLOW: No, he ain't coming any more today.

EASTON: Sides, who cares about him anyway?

CRASS: Or what if Rushton or Sweater come in for a look round?

(The men go back to work, but good naturedly, occasionally laughing, humming a song).

(The men sing)
Pull for the shore.

THE BEANO

(An Indian summer day. A waitress lays white table cloths over a long tressel table. A skittle game runs one side of the acting area. The men, Crass, Owen, Easton, Harlow, Philpott, and Sawkins, form a gauche group, silently watching the girl. They are dressed in their Sunday best. The girl turns, sees them, and drops a curtsey. One by one, they doff their hats. She exits. The group slowly breaks up)

HARLOW:*(quietly)* Bit of all right, eh?

EASTON: Not 'alf.

HARLOWE: If the meal's half as good.

EASTON: *(nodding)* Be allright.

CRASS: What the bleedin' hell you
whispering for? We in't in church
you know.

PHILP: Would be if Hunter had his way.

(bird song)

EASTON: What's that?

HARLOW: Sparrer.

PHILP: Sparrers don't sing. They cough
and spit. Like us.

OWEN: They sing out here.

EASTON: Any idea?

(They shake their heads, and listen)

CRASS: Ask me. I know's all about birds.

(Silence)

CRASS: Ask me.

(Silence)

CRASS: Them's a couple of lovely tits
is them.

(Philpott laughs, Harlow smiles)

CRASS: Cuckoo. CUCKOO!!

PHILPOTT: Eh, they've got skittles.

*(Owen stretches in the sun. Harlow
undoes his collar).*

CRASS: I'll gi's you a game.

(Philpott sets up)

OWEN: Might as well.

CRASS: *(to Easton)* Anybody got a fag?

EASTON: Have one of mine.

CRASS: Won' say no. Need a smoke.

PHILPOTT: Aye, all this fresh air can't be
good for you.

SAWKINS: *(laughing)* Tits!

(Easton crosses to the table)

EASTON: *(Softly)* What's all these
knives and forks for?

OWEN: God knows. Just keep eating
until you run out.

EASTON: Then tear in with your bare
hands.

OWEN: Something like that.

HARLOW: It's our meal. If you want
it all wrapped in paper, you could
have it. We've paid for it.

*(The waitress returns with another bowl
of flowers)*

CRASS: Thirsty work this standing
about.

OWEN: He should know.

CRASS: *(to Philpott)* Couple of little
tits just flown by.

PHILPOTT: Gi' up, Bob.

CRASS: Are we, or are we not, s'pposed
to be enjoying ourselves?

PHILPOTT: We are. We are, yes.

(Sawkins groans)

HARLOW: Sawkins gone a nice shade
of green.

OWEN: Matches the grass.

EASTON: Been sinkin' 'em like there's
no tomorrow.

HARLOW: Perhaps there in't.

CRASS: Here, darling —

WAITRESS: Yes, sir.

19

CRASS: Me men is thirsty. Hot weather an' all.

WAITRESS: Oh, yes.

CRASS: Have to look after them then, you see. Make sure they 'ave a good time. I'm their coddy, you see.

WAITRESS: I forgot. I'm sorry.

(She takes the towel off that is covering a barrel of beer).

CRASS: Lo and Behold!

PHILPOTT: Should keep us going for a bit.

WAITRESS: I put the towel over to keep it cool.

CRASS: Lovely. I'll see you alright. I'll have a word wi' your boss before I go.

WAITRESS: Shall I take the orders?

CRASS: I've seen one of these before. Don't fret.

WAITRESS: Sorry I forgot.

PHILPOTT: It's just to take the sweat off us, miss.

CRASS: We're open.

PHILPOTT: How do we pay for this?

WAITRESS: It's all in.

CRASS: All in, eh? Sounds a bargain *(blows her a kiss)* I'll have a pint first though, eh?

WAITRESS: Better get on.

(she exits)

PHILPOTT: You embarrass the kid.

CRASS: They know their way round. Woun't be working here else. Let's get to work, eh?

(The two of them pour pints, Philpott handing them to the men).

SAWKINS: Where's mine?

PHILPOTT: It's coming. Just get sat down before you fall. Will, gi'him a hand.

EASTON: Right.

SAWKINS: Lookin' for a fight, eh?

EASTON: Come on.

SAWKINS: Square up. *(Easton plays the 'fight')* Stop 'opping about.

PHILPOTT: Ding. End of round one. To your corner.

(They get Sawkins to the table)

SAWKINS: In the blue corner . . . I woun't have hurt you, you know.

EASTON: No.

HARLOW: Free booze, eh? This is the life, innit?

OWEN: Could be.

HARLOW: Don't start.

OWEN: What?

HARLOW: You know.

OWEN: *(smiling)* Not a peep.

HARLOW: Let's have one day wi'out it, eh?

EASTON: I'm for that.

OWEN: My solemn word. Not a word about — you know what.

EASTON: As a gentleman.

OWEN: That wouldn't be worth much, would it?

HARLOW: Now then.

OWEN: My solemn word as a worker.

HARLOW: I'll buy that.

PHILPOTT: You can't buy nothing today. It's all free. Here you are, mate.

(He places a pint in front of Sawkins)

SAWKINS: Ah!

(He passes out. His head banging on the table)

EASTON: Is he all right?

PHILPOTT: Thank God, it was only his head. Thick as two planks.

HARLOW: Let him sleep it off 'til dinner.

(The noise of the skittles occasionally stirs Sawkins, who lifts his head, gazes at the pint, and gives it up as a bad job)

CRASS: *(Belches: proudly)* Mating call of the big-breasted tit.

HARLOW: *(laughing)* Who let the bull in?

PHILP: *(to Owen)* Watch out with that red tie.

CRASS: Where's me ball?

PHILP: Only got one, 'ave you?

CRASS: *(smiling)* Dirty bugger.

PHILP: *(hands him the 'cheese)* Say cheese.

CRASS: Smile for the birdie.

PHILP: It's called a cheese.

CRASS: Don't have to tell me.

PHILP: You score?

HARLOW: Right.

CRASS: Don't you trust me?

PHILP: Far as I can throw you.

OWEN: How's the wife?

EASTON: Due any time.

OWEN: What do you want?

EASTON: Lad. No world for women is it?

OWEN: Should be.

EASTON: My dad come off the land round here.

OWEN: What was it like?

EASTON: Never talked about it. When I was a kid I used to ask him to go out for the day. Fishin'. Mind you, in't the time, is there? But it always stuck in the back of me mind.

CRASS: *(having thrown)* Fucking thing won't go down.

PHILP: You should be so lucky.

(Sawkins wakes up with sound of the game)

SAWKINS: Where's mine?

(he collapses again)

OWEN: There must be a stream down there, where that line of trees is.

EASTON: Belong to somebody won't it?

OWEN: Could belong here. Ask the landlord. He might have a line.

CRASS: First go. That was a warm up.

PHILP: Stone me.

EASTON: That'd be someat, would it? Goin' fishing.

HARLOW: You'll miss your dinner.

EASTON: Oh, ye'. Don't want to miss me dinner.

OWEN: Ask em. They might pack someat up for you.

EASTON: You fancy coming?

OWEN: Maybe stroll down later.

HARLOW: I'll stick by the oasis.
(empties glass)

OWEN: Take Bert wi' you.

CRASS: So long as he don't take the barrel.

OWEN: Ask em.

EASTON: Bugger me if I don't think I will.

(he exits)

(Crass is preparing to throw the 'cheese' or ball. He belches again).

CRASS: Flyin' low these tits. *(laughs)*

PHILP: Where did you learn to do that?

CRASS: Years of practise.

PHILP: You should go on the stage.

CRASS: Thought about it.

PHILP: There's a bloke in France who does a turn where he farts tunes.

CRASS: Get away.

PHILP: Strike me dead. Plays the French National anthem — Marshall Hayes — all on a fart. All the different notes. Everything. Gets paid a fortune for stinking the place out.

HARLOW: Like Hunter.

CRASS: Steady on.

PHILP: He's knocking the shorts back in't he?

CRASS: He's tea total. Shining Light Chapel.

PHILP: Sweater is an all. But I seen em both, sliding up to the bar at the Queen Elizabeth's. You watch 'em.

CRASS: You reckon he earns a lot of money?

PHILP: Who? Hunter?

CRASS: No. This farter.

PHILP: Sweater.

CRASS: Give over. This bloke what plays tunes. Bum-diddy-bum-bum.

PHILP: Not 'arf.

CRASS: I could do that.

PHILP: That's why the table's outside.

CRASS: I could. I could play the National Anthem.

PHILP: In French?

CRASS: Don't be daft. I'm a Tory. I Don't play the Frogs bloody anthem. What do you bet?

HARLOW: We believe you.

CRASS: Come on. Money where your mouth is. What do you bet?

HARLOW: Pint of ale.

CRASS: You're on.

HARLOW: Wi' a bit of luck he might blow himself away.
(Philp winks at the men)

CRASS: Show you who's top dog round here. Hold me coat.

PHILP: What's the medley?

CRASS: God Save the King.

(Crass screws up his face and prepares for action)

PHILP: You'll burst a gut.

(Bert runs on. He stops in front of Crass)

BERT: You all right, Mr Crass?

(Crass deflates dramatically)

PHILP: It's a game, Bert.

BERT: Oh.

(Bert crosses over to Owen and Harlow)

CRASS: Bleedin' kid. I'll kill him.

CRASS: I was all set.

PHILP: No doubt about it. I'll get you a drink.

CRASS: Should bloody well think so.

OWEN: Where you been?

BERT: They let you go over all the shop here.

MARLOW: How's dinner goin'?

BERT: Be any time.

HARLOW: All I need for a perfect day.

CRASS: My stomach's rumbling.

PHILP: What tune?

CRASS: I'll think of something.

PHILP: Better concentrate on the game. I'm winning.

OWEN: What's it like?

BERT: I've been in the kitchen. Got white tiles everywhere. And it's spotless, spotless as anything I've ever seen. Be good to work on a place like this, woun't it?

OWEN: Lots of craft in these places. Lots of jobs we couldn't handle now.

PHILP: Top up.

OWEN: Not for me.

CRASS: Twist me arm.

HARLOW: I'll get 'em. You want one, kid?

BERT: Ye'.

HARLOW: Just a taste, eh?

(Philpott throws his last)
(alternative dialogue if Philpott wins —)
PHILP: That'll teach you.
CRASS: Best out of three?
PHILP: Enough for me. *(or—)*
PHILP: I gi' you this game.
CRASS: No stopping me. You on, Frank?

OWEN: Why not?

CRASS: You know the rules?

OWEN: No punching below the belt.

CRASS: See you've played before.

(They begin a new game)
(Easton returns, carrying a fishing rod, and two bags)
EASTON: Look at this then eh? it's the Landlord's own. He's borrowed it us.

CRASS: That's a good un. Couple of bob there. I know. Used to be a champion when I was a kid.

PHILP: Savin' old boots from drownin'.

CRASS: Sight more use than piddlin' fish.

PHILP: You got me there.

CRASS: Gi' us a go. I'll show you.

HARLOW: Don't take it off him.

CRASS: I was just goin' to learn him.

23

BERT: You know what to do, do you?

EASTON: Course I do.

CRASS: Let's see you then.

(Easton, with the aid of an endless stream of useless advice from the men, practices a few casts).

BERT: He goin' fishing?

OWEN: You want to go?

BERT: Can I?

EASTON: Ye' Nip in. Tell em to pack you up.

BERT: Right.

EASTON: See you down by the trees.

(Bert exits)

CRASS: Come on, smart arse.
(Easton practises a cast)
CRASS: No, you throw it over your shoulder.

PHILPOTT: Stand back, 'for he blinds you.

HARLOW: Let some line out.

EASTON: Like this.

OWEN: Just mind me.

EASTON: Here we go.

HARLOW: The weight'll take the line out.

CRASS: Gi' it a good flick.
(he casts again)

PHILP: Well, he should certainly frighten the buggers to death, if nothing else.

CRASS: *(looking in a bag)* What's in here?

EASTON: Worms.

PHILP: That's your first course settled. What's for puddin'?

EASTON: No They're packing us up proper *(loads gear)* See you lads later.
(He exits)

CRASS: Gi' us a quick go, eh? *(Pause)*

Miserable fucker. Can't tell 'em ought. *(He returns to the game)*

CRASS: Pint on this one, is there?

OWEN: Make it two.

CRASS: *(grinning)* Good for you. Right.
(They go back to the game. Philpott scores).
(Harlow sits and lights his pipe)
(Crass throws, walks down for the ball)

OWEN: How many's that?

PHILP: Won't lookin!

(Crass kicks a few more down)

CRASS: Six!

PHILP: You lying bugger.

OWEN: You'd cheat your grandma, you would.

CRASS: Honest! They were on the wobble.

(The waitress enters with the soup dishes)

WAITRESS: It'll be any minute now. Just waiting for the rest of your party to finish in the lounge.

HARLOW: We've waited an whole year. A few minutes more won't make a lot of difference.

WAITRESS Not been here before?

HARLOW: I think it's the first year for any of us.

24

WAITRESS: Nice, in't it?

HARLOW: Ye', I think we'll be back. Touch wood.
(She smiles and lays the table. Harlow lies back in the sun. The men play the game. Hunter [Easton] enters, a glass in one hand. He stands, surveying the scene, unnoticed by the men. He crosses to Harlow and casts his shadow across him. Harlow opens his eyes, and, startled, is about to leap to his feet, but resists it. Hunter continues staring at him. Reluctantly, Harlow rises to his feet. Hunter walks and stands by the end of the table).

PHILP: He's here.

CRASS: Come on, let's finish the game off.

PHILP: Don't keep him waiting.

CRASS: Just when I'm winning.

OWEN: Get some food inside us.

CRASS: Bloody good idea.

PHILP: *(waking Sawkins up)* Come on. Dinner.

SAWKINS: 'Bout bloody time an' all.
(The men move to the table, jockeying for position as far away from Hunter as possible. The waitress exits).

CRASS: Done us proud, an't they, Mr. Hunter?

HUNTER: The gentlemen are hindulging in their repast on the shade of the verandah. They will honour us after dinner for the cigars etcetra.

PHILP: Fair enough.

HARLOW: Who cares a monkeys?

(The men sit)

PHILP: I'm ready for what ever they can throw at me.

CRASS: Been starvin' meself all year just for this.

(Hunter is still standing. Crass rises, signals grace to the other men, and reluctantly they all rise).

HUNTER: A few words. A few words of spiritual substenance to enhance our physical substenance, that is, the splendid meal what we are about to partake off.

CRASS: Hear! Hear!

HUNTER: *(As the waitress arrives with the soup)* Moment. *(She stands as confused as the men)* Today is a special day. Not just because it is the annual worker's Beano, but also because it is Whit.

PHILP: What?

HUNTER: Pentecost. He has risen from the dead and gone to sit on the right hand at the great table in Heaven, vouchsafed for his followers to be visited by the Holy Ghost. In this house. That they are all in. Then. Yes.

THE MEN: Amen.

(They start to sit, as Hunter continues. A note of rebellious hysteria begins to affect them).

HUNTER: And when the day of Pentecost was fully come, they were all with one accord in one place. And suddenly there came a sound from heaven as of a rushing mighty wind, and it filled the house where they were sitting.

(Philpott points at Crass, laughing)

HUNTER: And there appeared unto them eleven tongues like as of fire, and it sat upon each of them. And they were filled with the Holy Ghost, and began to speak with other tongues, as the Spirit gave them utterance.

(He gazes skywards. The men say Amen, and sit)

HUNTER: Sit thou on my right hand.

PHILP: No chance.

HUNTER: Until I make thy foes thy footstool.

(The waitress begins to serve the soup. Hunter looks down, sees the men).

CRASS: Very good, Mr. Hunter, sir. Very good.

HUNTER: Yes. For what we are about to receive may the Lord make us truly thankful.

CRASS: Amen.

PHILP: Hear! hear!
(Hunter sits. Blackout)

ACT TWO

A TIME FOR SPEECHES

(The men sit, collars, waistcoats undone, the remnants of a gargantuan feast in front of them. They smoke giant cigars. At a smaller round table the masters sit. A group of indolent, life-like marionettes. Laughter and talk).

CRASS: *(Rising)* Gentlemen, as Secretary of the Beano Outings Committee, I gi' you the breakdown of the financial situation. As follows. Men paid in five bob each. Boy we allowed in half-price making total of –

HUNTER: Thirty seven shillings and sixpence.

CRASS: Thirty seven shillings and sixpence. Mr Rushton has kindly given 10/- towards the expenses.
(Cheers) Our Mayor, Mr Sweater, who's house we has the privilege of doing up 5/- *(Cheers)* and our guests, Mr Grinder, Mr Lettum, Mr Didlum and Mr Toonarf half-a-crown each, making a total of –

HUNTER: Three pounds two shillings and sixpence.

CRASS: Three pounds two shillings and sixpence. Also we wrote letters to the firms what supply us with . . . er . . . supplies, and asked them to cough up something: one of them sent half-a-crown, another two shillings, and so on, and two wrote back saying that things are cut so fine nowadays that they din't hardly make no profit on their stuff, so they couldn't afford to chip in. But all together their total was seven shillings and sixpence – making a total to –

HUNTER: Three pounds ten shillings.

CRASS: Three pounds ten shillings. Now dinner was four shillings per man.

HUNTER: One pound twelve shillings.

CRASS: Two coaches. Ten bob each.

HUNTER: One pound.

CRASS: Total cost –

HUNTER: Two pounds twelve.

CRASS: Two pounds twelve, leaving a profit of –

HUNTER: Eighteen shillings.

CRASS: Eighteen shillings to be shared among the men, which works out at

HUNTER: Two and nine per man, One and six for the boy.

CRASS: Right.

(Round of applause)

PHILP: I'd like to move a hearty thanks for all the good work of the committee.
(Cries of hear, hear, etc.)

(Hunter rises to his feet)

HUNTER: I believe everyone will agree with me, when I say that they should not let the occasion pass without drinking the health of their esteemed and respected employer, Mr Rushton. *(Hear. Hear)* It is not necessary for me to say much in praise of Mr Rushton, you know him as well as I do myself and to know him is to esteem him. Much pleasure in asking you to drink Mr Rushton's health.

(They all rise)

CRASS: Musical honours, chaps.

(They sing: For he's a jolly good fellow. .)

(From the spare seat, Rushton rises)

RUSHTON: Thank you. I've been in business now for nearly sixteen years, and this is, I believe, the eleventh annual outing I have had the pleasure of attending. During all that time the business has steadily progressed and developed, and I hope the progress made in the past will continue in the future. Of course, I realise that the success of the business depends very largely upon you, the men, as well as upon myself. I do my utmost to try to get you work, and it's necessary — if the business is to grow and prosper — that you should also do your best to get the work done when I have secured it for you. The masters cannot do without the men, and the men cannot do without the masters. *(Hear. Hear)* It's a simple matter of division of labour. The men work with their hands, the masters with their brains, and one is no use without the other. I sincerely hope that the the good feeling that has hitherto existed between myself and you, the workers, will always continue, and I thank you for the way which you have responded to the toast to my health. Thank you.

(Crass rises)

CRASS: I ain't goin' to make a long speech, cos I ain't much of a speaker, but I feel sure you will all hagree with me when I says that — next to Mr Rushton — there ain't nobody the men have more respect and liking for than Mr Hunter here. So I begs to propose the health of Mr Hunter.

(Applause. Musical Honours)
(Hunter Rises)

HUNTER: Thank you for that kindness. Hope I deserve your goodwill. Always tried to be fair. Considerate. To all men. *(to waitress)* Kindly replenish the men's glasses.

(He waits until their glasses are filled again)

HUNTER: Now propose the health of our distinguished guests. So kindly contributed to the expenses. Mr Sweater, Mr Grinder, Mr. Didlum, Mr Toonarf. And to wish Mr Sweater good luck in the coming elections.

(Loud cheers and appaluse).

(Mr Sweater [Sawkins] rises)

CRASS: Floor for Mr Sweater. Order in the house please.

SWEATER: Unaccustomed as I am to public speaking *(some of the men laugh)* No, I'm not going to make a big speech, just to say how much pleasure it has given myself and my colleagues to join with you on your outing, and to be able in some way to help bring it about. It's very gratifying to see the good feeling that exists between Mr Rushton and his men, which is of course only how it should be, because masters and men are fellow workers — one with his brains, the others with their hands. Both workers, and therefore their interests are the same. I like to see the master doing his best for his men, and the men realising that he's not only a master, but also a friend. Master and men pulling together, doing their best, realising that their interest is identical. If only all masters and men would do this, we'd all soon see that everything would work out, that there would be more work and less poverty. Yes, let the masters do their best for

27

their men, and the men for their masters and they would soon enough discover that was the true solution of the social problems, and not the silly nonsense talked by people who go around waving red flags. *(Cheers)*. Most of those sorts are chaps who are too lazy to work their livin'.

MEN: Hear. Hear.

SWEATER: Now you can take it from me as one who knows, if ever these socialists get the upper hand there'll just be a few of the hartful dodgers who will get the cream, and there'll be nothing left but 'ard work for the rest. That's what all these agitators are after — they want you to keep them in idleness. Well, finally, on behalf of my colleagues I thank you for your kind wishes and hope to see you on many more such occasions in the future.

(Loud cheers from some of the men. Crass jibes at Owen, who remains silent).

CRASS: What you got to say to that then, eh?

SAWKINS: He ant got ought to say now.

CRASS: Come on, get up and make a speech.

SAWKINS: Not a peep.

(Sweater rises to his feet again)

SWEATER: When I made the remarks that I did, I din't know there was any socialists here. I could tell from the look of you that most of you had more sense. At the same time I'm glad I said what I did, because it just shows what sort of chaps these Socialists are. They're pretty artful — they know when to talk and when to keep their mouths shut. What they like is nothing better than getting hold of a few ignorant workin' men in their workshop or public house, and then they can talk by the mile — regular shop lawyers, you know what I mean — I'm right and everyone else is wrong.

(Cheers from the men)

SWEATER: When they find themselves in the company of heducated people who know a little bit more than they do, and who are not likely to be misled by a lot of claptrap, why then, mum's the word. So next time you hears any of these shop lawyers arguments, you'll know how much it is worth.

(He sits down. Crass, delighted, starts up a song of:—

CRASS:
Now, I'm not a wealthy man
But I've hit upon a plan
That will render you
As happy as a king
And if you will allow,
I'll sing it to you now,
For time you know is
Always on the wing.

(Chorus: The men and Sweater join in)

Work, boys, work and be contented
So long as you've enough to buy a meal
Ev'ry man you may rely
Will be wealthy bye and bye
If you'll only put your shoulder to the wheel.

(The chorus is repeated while Crass borrows Sweater's cane, ties a white handkerchief round it, throws the flowers from the vase in front of Owen onto the floor, and sticks the white flag in it)..

CRASS: If I can find a duck, I'll let you have the four feathers an' all.

(Silence. Owen does not speak. Crass begins to laugh. Sullenly Harlow stands. Crass sits down. Harlow takes the 'flag' from the vase. Silence).

HARLOW: We come here today as friends, and we want to forget all our differences, and enjoy ourselves for a couple of hours. But seeing how Mr Sweater has started it, and now all this (indicates the flag) going on, well, it warrants some answer, does this. First off, socialists are lazy. I've heard this time in, time out. Well, let me say, I've worked wi' 'em, and if they're lazy the rest of us is bone-idle.

It's all right calling 'em, that's easy done, But you've got to attack what they believe in. I should like to have heard that, instead of just painting 'em black. The men work with their hands, the masters with their brains. That's been drummed in to me so much I can't hardly see what's at the end of me fingers. Not just hands.But work. I've served my time and I know. Your work in't made wi' your hands, it's made with your brains, planning, thinking all the time. If that wasn't a fact, you'd employ the loonies from the workhouse on all our jobs. You could get them cheaper, 'stead of just locking them up. You don't, because they can't use their brains in any job. You talk of the master as being a friend — how can he be, even if he wanted to be. He's got got to compete with all the other firms. He's got to undercut them — so he's got to sweat his workers for as little as possible. We're not the same. Our aims are not the same. You get old, and rich and fat. And when you retire, you've got something to sell up for your old age, and something to leave your kids. What have we got? We own no more at the end than we did at the beginning, and that's nothing. Our health is probably buggered, and we're thrown onto the rubbish tip, onto charity, into the workhouse. No. Our aims arc different from yours. I've put it off and put it off but it's there like a wall I keep banging me nose on. Your aim is to keep what you've got. Our aim is to make a world where anyone's kids won't come to want. Where there's freedom . . . It has to be said. *(He unties the handkerchief and passes it to Crass.*

He lays the stick gently down on the table and sits down).

CRASS: We an't come here to listen to a load of political speeches, as we, lads?

PHILP: No. Come on, let's get the old joanna going, eh? Eh, Bob, come on, you can still knock out a tune. Can we play that miss?

WAITRESS: 'course you can.

PHILP: Gentleman and lady, I give you the mighty minim, bungling Bob Crass. He's got a good left hand this kid. Mind you, it's where his right hand should be, but not to worry. Gentlemen, I reckon we may be able to persuade the lady here to give us a tune.

(As Philpott talks to her, Sawkins swings spontaneously into the chorus)

SAWKINS:
Put me amongst the girls.
Put me amongst the girls.
Do me a favour do.
You know I'd do as much for you.
Put me amongst the girls.
Those with the curly curls.
They'll enjoy themselves, And so will I.
If you put me amongst the girls.

(He collapses)

PHILP: What are you going to sing, miss?

WAITRESS: Won't you buy my pretty flowers.

(She takes the stand. Philpott gives her the bunch of flowers that Crass has thrown down).

PHILP: Well she's got to have something to sell.

WAITRESS:
Underneath the gaslights glitter,
Stands a little fragile girl,
Heedless of the night wind bitter,
As they round about her whirl,
While the undreds pass unheeding,
In the evening's waning hours,
Still she cries with tearful pleading,
Won't you buy my pretty flowers?

There are many, sad and weary,
In this pleasant land of ours,
Crying every night, so dreary,
Won't you buy my pretty flowers?

Not a loving word to cheer her,
From the passer-by is heard,
Not a friend to linger near her.

With a heart by pity stirred,
Homeward goes the tide of fashion,
Seeking pleasure's pleasant bow'rs,
None to hear with sad compassion,
Won't you buy my pretty flowers?

(Chorus)

(During the last chorus, Philpott quietly takes the hat round the men)

PHILP: Well, I'm not going to crack a joke about that. That was lovely that was. And now the men have asked me if you would accept this small remuneration from all of us for how you have looked after us today? Right, now it's my turn.

HUNTER:
Joy! because the circling year,
Brings our day of blessing here:
Day when first the light divine,
On the church began to shine.

(Owen laughs)

Like to quivering – er –

Like to quivering – tongues of flame

(He has forgotten it. He sits down. Some of the men laugh, others just pull faces. Philpott sings Two Lovely Black Eyes, the men quickly join in).

PHILPOTT:
Strolling so happy down Bethnal Green,
This gay youth you might have seen,
Tompkins and I, with his girl between,
Oh, What a surprise!
I praised the Conservatives frank and free,
Tompkins got angry so speedily,
All in a moment he handed to me,
Two lovely black eyes!

Two lovely black eyes!
Oh! What a surprise!
Only for telling a man he was wrong,
Two lovely black eyes!

Next time I argues I thought it best,
To give the Conservative side a rest,
The merits of Gladstone I freely pressed,
Then, oh! What a surprise!
The chap I had met was a Tory blue,
Nothing the Liberals right could do,
This was my share of the argument too,

Two lovely black eyes.

(Chorus)

The moral you've caught I can hardly doubt,
Never on politics rave and shout,
Leave it to others to fight out
If you would be wise.
Better, far better it is to let,
Liberals and Tories alone, you bet,
Unless you're willing and anxious to get,
Two lovely black eyes!

(Chorus)

THE RETURN FROM THE BEANO

(The men form into two coaches. The front one has the Brigands, the back one Crass and the drunks. They sing the chorus of Two Lovely Black Eyes.)

PHILP: *(blowing on horn)* Two fucking lovely black eyes. Two fucking lovely black eyes etc.

CRASS: What if Mr Rushton were to hear you.

SAWKINS: Fuck Rushton.

CRASS: If he find's out you're swearing like that he'll sack you both.

SAWKINS: And fuck you too Crass. Don't you tell us not to swear. You're as bad as Hunter and Rushton together.

CRASS: No, I'm not.

SAWKINS: Yes you are. You're nothing but a bleeding toe-rag.

PHILP: Who's fucking idea was it, one man one room.

CRASS: It weren't me.

PHILP: Yes it were.

CRASS: No, it weren't

SAWKINS: Knock him off his perch.

(As they get more violent, the coach is getting faster and faster, chasing the one in front. Blackout).

(They form into different coaches – the front one with Hunter, Rushton, and Sweater, the back one with Harlow, Crass, Owen and Bert. The front coach sing 'Where is My Wandering Boy Tonight' verse and chorus. Hunter cries at the end. Harlow sings one verse and chorus of 'Break the News to Mother').

THE END OF WORK ON THE CAVE

(The men are working frantically on the final touches of the house. Bert is careering about with trestles loading the cart. Hunter [Sawkins] is in the house. He watches Owen who is putting the last touches to the Moorish Room).

HUNTER: Seven books. Seven books over the estimate. Ten and sixpence. What profit, eh? Three coats. Once in a blue moon thank god. Three weeks he said. Four. Four weeks. Glad to see the back of this one. Fancy work. You'll want to sign it next. Hartists. Money has to come from somewhere you know. Not manna from heaven.

OWEN: There's a couple of sheets of gold left over. You'd better have them.

(Hunter takes them holding them out on the palm of his hand. He stares at them).

HUNTER: 'ave you back on the brush Monday.
(He turns to Bert)

HUNTER: Seven. Get me the seven penny men.

BERT: Yes, Mr Hunter, sir.

(Bert runs around the house)

BERT: He wants you up in the drawing room.

PHILP: What for?

BERT: Dunno.

HARLOW: He woun't call us up for a slaughter.

PHILP: He'd just pass the word to Crass.

(Easton joins them)

HARLOW: You must be right, 'bout what you 'eard.

EASTON: What?

HARLOW: What you heard. More work.

EASTON: Oh ye'.

PHILP: Why would be call us up though? He could just as well tell Crass.

HARLOW: Soon find out.

(The men enter the drawing-room. Hunter stares at the gold. They exchange glances with Owen. Silence).

PHILP: Nice.

HUNTER: Don't pay for your opinion. You men all gets sevenpence an hour?

PHIL/HARLOW: Yes, sir.

(Easton nods).
OWEN: I –

HUNTER: Hartwork. Ha'penny more. That's done now.

OWEN: Yes.

HUNTER: Seven pence.

HARLOW: I've never worked under price yet.

PHILP: Nor me neither.

HUNTER: Well, you can please your-selves. But as of starting on the new job, we's decided not to pay more than six-and a-half. Things is cut so fine now we can't afford to pay seven pence no longer. Just clear up here, get down the shop and we'll pay you up. But don't bother comin' in on Monday morning, less you's willin' to take six and a half. Please yourselves. Take it or leave it.

(He leaves. The men stand, confused)

HARLOW: He can't do that.

PHILP: He's just done it.

HARLOW: We can't take six and a half lying down.

EASTON: What can you do?

PHILP: Seven's the bottom for skilled men. It's hard enough making a go on that, ne' mind six and a half.

(Sawkins helps clear up the house).

HARLOW: And what if it don't stop there?

PHILP: We'll end up like Sawkins working for five.

HARLOW: Or like Bert, slaving our guts out for nothing but bad air.

EASTON: Bert's apprentice though, in't he? He's getting trained up.

HARLOW: How much training did they give you?

PHILP: You do the training so you come out and get skilled rate. That's what you gi' your years up for. The rate. If you go cutting back what's the point?

EASTON: I'm not disagreeing.

HARLOW: Got to stop the rot somewhere, or it makes a mock of your whole life.

PHILP: People go working below rate they cut all our throats.

HARLOW: Show me the buggers.

PHILP: What we goin' to do then.

HARLOW: We're not goin' to take it. That's what we're goin' to do. He can't do wi'out us. If we all stand together, he'll have to back down.

PHILP: He's got to have the skilled men.

HARLOW: Right.

OWEN: Do you know what you're saying?

HARLOW: We're talking unions, aren't we? I might have been pissed at the Beano, but I ain't goin' back on everything I said. I don't go all the way wi' you by a long chalk, but if we band together, we can bargain. I can see that.

PHILP: Can't take everything they throw at you, can you?

HARLOW: Right.

OWEN: Look, there's more than that, though. Right. We band together, but not just for bargaining. That can only work while we have something to bargain with. While they need our labour. As soon as they don't, then we're out in the snow. Take it on a bit further. Band together to take it back from them. Don't wait for when they don't need us. We don't need them. Let's band together not to bargain but to own.

PHILP: Steady on. I'm only talking about a a'penny.

HARLOW: Right. Might have a chance to get that but we ain't goin' to get castles in Spain. What we've got to do is stop the bugger cutting us. Ne' mind what might happen in fifty years. If he keeps cutting the rate we won't make next year, and neither will our kids.

PHILP: We're not navvies he can pick up anywhere. We're skilled.

OWEN: Stop dividing yourself off from them. Once we do that we're lost. We're not fighting for the crumbs between ourselves. You've got to go for the whole loaf. Any other way they'll have you.

(Crass arrives)

CRASS: Come on, Bert, get this bleedin' thing loaded up.

HARLOW: Listen, Frank, are you with us?

OWEN: Am I with you?

HARLOW: Yes.

OWEN: Yes. Of course I am.

HARLOW: Right. We all walk in the office when we get back the shop, and tell him.

PHILP: Ye'.

HARLOW: You in, Easton?

PHILP: Course he is. He's got a kid on the way.

CRASS: *(entering)* What the bloody 'ells goin' on here?

HARLOW: Hunter's tryin' to cut our rate.

CRASS: What? Did he say ought about mine?

PHILP: He won't touch yours.

CRASS: What's he goin' to?

PHILP: Six and a half.

CRASS: Bad luck, lads.

HARLOW: It in't bad luck at all. We're all goin' marching down there to have it out with him.

CRASS: And he'll sack the lot of you.

PHILP: He can't do wi'out us. He'll not get skilled men to work at that price. He's just trying it on.

CRASS: Well, I wish the three of you good luck, and I'll come see you in the workhouse.

HARLOW: Four of us.

CRASS: Who's the four?

HARLOW: Me. Joe, Frank and Will.

CRASS: Don't talk daft. Will's already on six and a half.

(Silence)

HARLOW: Is that right?

EASTON: I've got a kid on the way.

HARLOW: I've got four kids and they're goin' to be that much poorer for the likes of you.

CRASS: Let's get this cart loaded then, eh?

EASTON: Right.

(Easton and Crass leave the room)

EASTON: What did you go and say that for?

CRASS: Sorry, mate. Won't thinking. Din't mean to land you in it. Anyroad if you'd gone wi' Frank and Harlow you'd been a sight worse off.

EASTON: Maybe.

CRASS: I've got a little job on this afternoon. Down the shop. Worth a couple of bob. Are you interested?

EASTON: I don't know.

33

CRASS: You're not doing me any favours. Just thought I'd offer it you first.

EASTON: Thanks.

CRASS: Be worth a drink down the Cricketers.

EASTON: I'll see you all right.

CRASS: No need.

(They continue to load the cart, with Sawkins and Bert).

PHILP: Can't stand here all day.

HARLOW: Bastard.

PHILP: I'd 'ave been tempted to do the same. Kid on the way. No good taking it out on him, is it? If it won't him it'd be somebody else.

HARLOW: You can' trust nobody.

OWEN: That's not true.

PHILP: For all we know you know, there may be no money. Just 'cos Hunter's a bleeder don't mean he aint telling the truth when he says Rushton can't afford to pay no more.

OWEN: You really believe Rushton's a stone throw from the soup queue?

PHILP: Don't know what to believe. I see some sense in what you say, Frank, but what comes of it? Only bad feeling between the men. I don't like it. Things are bad enough without that.

HARLOW: They've got you everywhere you turn, an't they?

OWEN: Is that it then? Take your bat and ball and go home?

HARLOW: You can stick out if you want.

OWEN: What can I do on me own? The

battles we have to fight aren't won by one man.

(Philpott and Harlow leave the room. Owen follows them)

CRASS: *(to Easton)* Don't go waving flags about that job. Just stick around after we knock off.

(The cart is almost loaded. Bert is sweeping out. The men collect their coats and gear)

HARLOW: Look at this, eh? A place what would 'ave taken us four months to do a proper job, slapped on and done wi' in two..

PHILP: Aye. Plenty of work here if we had it done proper.

CRASS: Catch us up, Bert. Here's the keys.

(the cart moves off, Philpott, Harlow, Sawkins, and Owen steadying the load. Crass and Easton walking behind).

THE BRIGANDS TEA PARTY

(Grinder, Didlum, Lettum, Rushton and the Rev. Belcher enter the house. Sweater and his wife are standing in the Moorish room, In front of them is a giant tiered cake stand, and a table set for tea with expensive china.
The brigands collect and behold the Moorish Room).

MRS SWEATER: Welcome *(individually to all)*

LETTUM: Ah.

GRINDER: Tasteful. Tres tasteful. Always liked this 'ere Japanese style.

DIDLUM: Hardly what one calls Japanese. More your Chinese — or Egyptian.

MRS. SWEATER: Tea, Reverend Belcher.

BELCHER: Ta.

SWEATER: Moorish. Got the idear. Paris Exhibition. Sim'lar. Decoration. Halambra.

LETTUM: Ah.

MRS SWEATER: Tea, Mr Lettum.

LETTUM: Ta.

GRINDER: Foreign. Paris.

SWEATER: Palace. Sultan of Morocco.

GRINDER: Oh ah. I know.

MRS SWEATER: Tea, Mr Grinder.

GRINDER Wouldn't mind a cup. Ta.

SWEATER: Thought it'd make a nice drawing-room, Englishman's home. His castle. Mine to be a palace.

LETTUM: *(laughing)* Ah. Ah. Ah.

GRINDER: Very good. Very good.

MRS SWEATER: Mr Rushton

RUSHTON: Ta.

SWEATER: Cost a packet of course.

RUSHTON: Hands cost the earth.

MRS SWEATER: Mr Didlum

DIDLUM: Ta.

SWEATER: Expect to pay for class

MRS SWEATER: More tea, vicar?

(Belcher belches)

BELCHER: Ah.

MRS SWEATER: My husband and I. Pleased to see you. Very pleased. Please help yourself to teas. Please.

(During the remainder of the scene they help themselves to cakes, as Mrs Sweater also continually offers them, so that they are never without a number, which they balance and board about their person.

They eat fast, and grotesquely, mechanically, not hungrily).

RUSHTON: Nice and warm.

SWEATER: Log fire.

RUSHTON: Property paying, Mr. Lettum?

LETTUM: Always time for an increase.

(They laugh – Ah)

RUSHTON: Shops selling, Mr Didlum?

DIDLUM: Always need food, eh?

(They laugh – Ah! AH!)

SWEATER: Newspapers, Mr Grinder?

GRINDER: Same old story.

(They laugh – Ah! Ah! AH!)

MRS SWEATER: Muffin, vicar?

BELCHER: *(with a mouthful)* Butter runs down me collar.

MRS SWEATER: Shame.

GRINDER: I'm very fond of muffins.

MRS SWEATER: Muffin?

GRINDER: Ta. Paris Hexhibition meself. Looked at the moon through that big telescope. Never so surprised in me life. could see it quite plain and it's round.

DIDLUM: Course it's round. Din't think it was square, did you?

GRINDER: Always thought it was flat. Like a muffin.

SWEATER: Science is a wonderful thing.

GRINDER: Nice to stay abreast.

LETTUM: Ah.

GRINDER: Responsibility of leadership.

DIDLUM: Heavy weight.

RUSHTON: Heard a man say Hawstralia is underneath our feet. That's daft. Folk would drop off.

BELCHER: *(startled)* I'm awake.

SWEATER: If that was true, we ought to be able to walk on the ceiling of this room.

(They gaze skyward)

DIDLUM: Flies.

(They gaze downwards)

MRS SWEATER: Not in my house.

DIDLUM: No, but I have remarked flies. Walking on the ceiling.

RUSHTON: Flies is different. Flies have sticky feet.

GRINDER: Ah.

LETTUM: Talking of flies, recalls Councillor Weakling.

(They laugh)

LETTUM: Start again. Talking of science recalls conversation with Councillor Weakling. You know, he believes that we are hall descended from monkeys.

(More laughter)

LETTUM: Just you wait to hear how I knocked the wind out of him. *(Belcher farts)* After we had been arguing for a long time about what's called heverlotuion or some such, I ses to him, "Well', "I ses" I ses, "If it's true that we's all descended from monkeys, I think your family must have left orf where mine began".

(They chortle away merrily)

BELCHER: Personally, I'm on the side of the angels.

(In his merriment, he nearly chokes to death, with a mouthful of biscuits. They
rush to aid with cups of tea. Finally recovered—)

SWEATER: Mr Rushton

RUSHTON: *(coughs)* And now to work. Declare this secret meeting of the Mugsborough Council open. Lots to do. First, however, I think we should consider how best we can help our good friend, Mr Sweater here, in his campaign for election to Parliament. There can be no doubt in any of our minds that he will serve our interests in that office with the same dedication he has served them on the local level.

(Hear. Hear. The brigands sing 'Vote for Sweater, to the tune of Men of Harlech, under the scene).

RUSHTON: So I suggest we work out a plan of campaign. Then move on to local matters. It'll take a bit of time. But we must expect that. Running the world.

(Blackout).

(Easton stands, staring at a coffin. Crass is smiling).

EASTON: It's a coffin.

CRASS: Right first time.

EASTON: I thought it was a job like the others — paintin' venetian blinds or someat.

CRASS: Can't rely on them jobs, mate. Folks may not want you to do up their 'omes, but they still have to see their relatives off, don't they? Can't just leave them to peel away like the wallpaper. Come on, lift it up. You want to get in this side of the business. Always Plenty of Work.

(Bert is working on a child's wheelbarrow in Owen's house. Owen is painting a banner).

OWEN: Where did you get the wood, Bert?

BERT: It's firewood from the shop.
Hunter 'as me break it up for him
to take 'ome.

OWEN: Fire wood. 'Ave to paint it
red then, won't you?

BERT: *(laughing)* I was goin' to paint it
red, anyway.

*(Hunter is working late at the office. His
table is covered with sheets of paper.
There is a bottle there. His speech is
playing simultaneously with the
following Crass/Easton and Owen
scenes)*

HUNTER: Final reckoning. The Moorish
room. Hartists. 7½. 200 hours. Painter
100. 7. 1500. plus 700. 2200. 12
into. 166. 8 pence. 20, 8. 6. and 8. no.
7 for art now. 6½? Even 6½ no good
to me. Boy don't cost a penny, Fetch
and carry. 6½ no good to me. Got to
cut that. Boy, nothing. That's something.

OWEN: Nice dovetailing. Screws an' all,
eh?

BERT: Bought a bag of 'em.

OWEN: It's worth it.

HUNTER: Cost of materials. Why
Rushton coun't be done with gold
crown. Gold paint. Crowns of
gold. Gold leaf. Half a crown for
two, four a crown. Seven lamps
of fire. Seven men, 6½ now.

CRASS: Two shillings the fixing.
Shilling liftin' in. Five shillings the
funeral. We don't dig the hole.
We's skilled. We carries it. Do you
want the job or not?

HUNTER: Books. Fifteen. Twenty.
Forty elders with seven horns. Twenty
books of gold leaf with seven seals.
Gold plate. Gold leaf. Gold paint is
cheaper.

EASTON: Ye'

CRASS: Must be worth a pint.

EASTON: I'll see you all right.

CRASS: Nice thought. Now we'll need
some paint, to cover it up to walk
it through the streets. No need to do
the bottom no one'll see that. Go and
get some black paint.

HUNTER: Fifteen books at seven seals.
Fifteen books with seven seals, crowns
for four, eighteen and nine. Yes.
Measure of paper for a penny, and
three measures of barley for a penny.
See thou hurt not the oil and wine.
(pours himself a drink) Four beasts,
each with six wings. Six. Six. Six
penny men. Got to be. Six and a half.
No. Two and a half at six and a half.
Six and a half leaves of gold. Six and
half leaves nothing. Six seals. Six books
of four crowns of gold leaf.

(Philpott is with Owen and Bert).

PHILP: Should you be up?

OWEN: Course I should be up.

PHILP: You'll lay yourself up for good
if you go on like this. You've got to get
back in shape.

(Owen laughs)

PHILP: You're not goin' to survive
long just doin' the odd coffin plate
at a tanner a time.

OWEN: Nice to see you, Joe.

PHILP: It's a lot worse. in't it?

OWEN: What?

PHILP: Your asthma.

OWEN: The kid's not daft.

PHILP: Are you losin' blood?

OWEN: We're all of us losin' blood.

HUNTER: Then there's the paint. Blood red. Colours. Cartridge paper. More colours. Bloody Owen. Purple and scarlet colours, decked with gold leaf and precious stones and pearls and having a gold leaf in her hand full of abomination and filthiness of her fornication. Owen. Three coats of paint. Stirrer. Cover everything. One pound four for paint. No. One coat. Three coats. Warm walls. Boy nothing. Skirting. Wood worm. Wormwood. There would be wormwood. At Two Hundred thousand a star. No profit there. Two and a half. Where are you?

OWEN: Here's the plate. *(he hands a coffin plate to Phil)*

PHILP: Ta. I was thinking.

OWEN: Yes.

PHILP: Well, I know you din't see eye to eye with old Linden. But leaving politics aside. There'll be nobody there you see. Workhouse funerals. They just trot 'em out on the cart. Will and Bob'll be there. Will does the lift ins with Bob now.

OWEN: I'd heard.

PHILP: But they's sort of professional. Gettin' paid for it. Old Jack's been on me mind since Hunter gave him the boot. I gave him the baccy. Thought I'd take an 'our off and just square me self wi' him, you know. If you felt up to gettin' out a bit.

OWEN: When?

PHILP: Thursday. Ten o'clock.

OWEN: Fine.

PHILP: Nice work on the lettering.

OWEN: I put some time into it.

PHILP: I can see that.

OWEN: Not much though, is it?
 J. Linden, R.I.P.

PHILP: It's plenty. What more do you need than a name and a wish for peace?

(Silence)

OWEN: No. You're wrong. Joe. Your wish for peace chokes us all. Jokes us back to sleep, with your wish for peace. Ought for peace and quiet. And what we can't laugh off, we buy off with a whipround or a mumbled farewell. He was a good bloke for all his faults. And an absolution to forget. You take every pain from us, every death, every moment of panic. Let me tell you, Joe, when I die, you'll not find my grave. I'll still be kicking. There'll be no place for you to lay me down. I'll not be contained.

PHILP: Steady on, lad.

OWEN: You're a dangerous man, Joe. A jailer with generosity. Think, Joe, think.

PHILP: Take it easy. You do yourself no good.

OWEN: Joe

(Owen turns away. He is coughing. He faces Hunter. Philpott turns to Bert. Bert watches him. Philpott tries to shrug, and leaves).

HUNTER: Seven to 6 and a half. six and a half to six. What's six and a half to me? Six hundred pound for three hours. Unbelievable. Beast with seven horns six and a half horns and upon his head six and a half crowns and upon his hands the name of blasphemy. Hands.

CRASS: *(quietly smoking)* The bosses work with their brains. The men with their hands.

(Hunter cuts his wrists, and gazes at the blood).

HUNTER: And I saw one of his hands as it were wounded to death. He causeth all to receive a mark on their hands. Here is wisdom. Let him that hath under-standing count the number of the Beast. For it is the number of man. Six. Six

Six. Six hundred sixty shillings and sixpence. At two and a half per cent.

(He sits and stares at Owen, who turns back to his own room. Harlow stands, unloading a few vegetables from a small bag).

OWEN: You can't even feed your own.

HARLOW: Last of the allotment till Spring.

OWEN: Sell it. Gi' someat towards the rent.

HARLOW: Drop in the ocean to them. Lettum wants me on the street.

OWEN: I'm sorry.

HARLOW: What you sorry about? I said what I thought at the Beano. It was hightime.

OWEN: There's sixpence on the table there.

HARLOW: *(angry)* I'm givin' them you.

OWEN: Thank you.

HARLOW: You're no good to us dead.

OWEN: No?

(Crass had put on Hunter's hat and coat)

CRASS: Nice fit. Poor old Hunter. I allers said he was barmy. You can't 'ave a man in a responsible position what's round the bend. Men figure they can get away with blue murder when they see that.

HARLOW: I crawled to Crass for a job. He said what Hunter said after the Cave. Unreliable. Far fetched ideas. Can't employ a man what's unsound. Unsound? Me! I could have brained him.

OWEN: Why? He's right. We are unsound. Mentally. Must be, trying to convert a madhouse using only reason. Everyone

knows that's the last thing that's going to work a cure.

HARLOW: It's never bothered you before. Why now?

OWEN: I don't know what to do. I thought it would be so simple. Just tell them the truth. It's not difficult. A kid can follow it. They'd see it, and then they'd put it right.

HARLOW: Who's they?

CRASS: You keep in wi' me, Will. Might even make you coddy. Extra ha'penny Solve a few of your problems won't it?

EASTON: Ye', Bob.

CRASS: What?

EASTON: Mr. Crass.

HARLOW: Shake out of it, eh? It's just the beginning.

CRASS: Come on, set to. Lets get 'im underground, and done wi'. There's going to be a few changes round here.

(Crass and Harlow slowly carry the coffin out)

HARLOW: We're 'aving that public meeting now, top o' the hill. 'Cos if we get enough support, London say they may put up a Labour man. There's still time.

OWEN: Put up a Labour man?

HARLOW: Make the bleeder Sweater do a bit of sweating himself, if nothing else. And next time round we might even —

OWEN: When was that decided?

HARLOW: At the last meeting when you were laid up.

OWEN: It's a dead end. If we go into their game, if we enter their House of Parliament on the back of the Unions, they'll just buy us off. We've got to hold out for the works, not go for the crumbs. Even if we force Capitalism to eliminate poverty completely, the cancer will still be in the air. Dog will still eat dog. We've got to tear it out by the roots, and build a new world.

HARLOW: Just words, Frank. These *(He holds up a potato)* are more than words. These are what we are fighting for. If we can get you decent food, and a proper place to live, and get you work that in't crippling to your health, you'll live. Words won't gi' you that.

OWEN: To fix the energy of the workers on attacking symptoms instead of the root cause is at best stupid, and at worst − criminal.

HARLOW: We're all criminals are we?

OWEN: I'm not saying that.

HARLOW: That's exactly what you're saying. And what we are saying is let's do something. Let's get together, make sure the buggers don't cut our rate again, make sure you don't just get stuck in the workhouse. We've got a chance now. Let's take it. Are you coming with us or what?

OWEN: I'll have to think about it.

HARLOW: Listen, if we are going wrong you'd better be there to tell us. You're no good to man nor beast sitting in your pokey attic, waiting for death.

OWEN: In the midst of death there is life.

HARLOW: I'm not sure we can run to prophets.

OWEN: Make up your mind.

HARLOW: You make up yours. We're on the move, Frank. You with us or what?

OWEN: I'll come.

HARLOW: Thank God for that. Can we take the banner?

OWEN: It in't finished yet.

HARLOW: It in't a work of art, you know.

OWEN: *(smiling)* It is a work of art.

HARLOW: Come on. We need it now. Not tomorrow.
(Owen folds it up)

HARLOW: What you doing kid?

BERT: It's a wheelbarrow. For Easton's kid.

HARLOW: What you makin' Easton a present for?

OWEN: It's not for Easton. It's for the kid.

BERT: It's for Christmas.

HARLOW: But he's only a couple of months old.

BERT: Be there when he wants it though.

HARLOW: It's good.

BERT: It's not bad. Could do better. With the real materials.

OWEN: Catch us up will you?

BERT: Ye'. I'll just get it painted.
(Bert begins to paint the wheelbarrow)

(Owen and Harlow freeze. They turn. Workmen face them)

OWEN: Ready?

HARLOW: Yes.

(Owen raises the banner, on which is written Workers Unite. Harlow steps forward)

HARLOW: Brothers. Sisters. Comrades!

(As he paints the wheelbarrow Bert begins to sing softly)

BERT: Work for the day is coming
  Work in the night-time hours
  Work for the day is coming
  Work mid springing flowers.

(The company join in)

  Work while the dew is sparkling
  Work in the dawning sun
  Work for the day is coming
  When man's work is done!

(They hold the tableau as the lights fade to full. Blackout).

Afterword

For *Philanthropists*, we spent a month painting and decorating a disused warehouse in Plymouth. The mornings were devoted to painting, the afternoons to working on the play. Towards the end of the workshop, we improvised the works outing – the annual beano – that forms a central episode in Tressell's novel. As it turned out, the evening was to have a decisive influence on our vision of the play. Bill Gaskill, Peter Hartwell, the designer, the actors and myself were joined by Max Stafford-Clark and two of the builders working on the conversion of the warehouse – Fred the carpenter and Pete the paint. Our hosts were the students and staff of the Theatre Department at Dartington College. The following account is taken from letters I wrote during the workshop.

At lunch we raided Ross's, an ex-army surplus shop, and Oxfam, for old suits, shirts, to wear at the beano, went through the songs again, and the rough order of the scenes, dressed up and waited to be picked up in a van. We each took a character from the book which we were to 'play' for the evening. We were uncertain as to how things would work out at Dartington, in their beautiful dining-hall – all we planned was that we would have the meal, make the speeches and sing the song, and take it from there.

When we arrived, we were met at the main entrance to the Great Hall by an old lady who welcomed us to her hotel. We stood, confused by the splendour, desperately holding on to our hats, then entered the dining-room where four wenches, in white lace aprons, were waiting (these somewhat threw the improvisation for some of us by their sheer beauty). The lady at the door was, it turned out later, the wardrobe mistress; the girls, first-year drama students who had been told no more than to arrive and serve the mad Joint Stock their meal, in period Edwardian.

We sat down to dinner, the men at one end of a long table under the main chimney; Hunter (Chris Burgess) stranded, alone, at the far end. Rushton (Bill Gaskill) was in the middle of a second table, with some students and Grinder (Max Stafford-Clark) who appeared a little later, not in costume. The second table was taken up by college staff.

A barrel of beer had been laid on for the men and Hunter was apparently drinking lemonade which he obtained by slipping the waitress money.

The meal was soup, sausage and tomato pie with leeks and

potatoes, and a variety of desserts, jellies, etc. Oddly, characters began to slip from caricature to character (with only the occasional breakout) as the drink had its effect. It was relatively good-humoured among the men.

Then Hunter started the speech, and Chris really did look like the description in the book. Crass (Fred Pearson) gave the accounts, and the surplus to be given out among the men was greeted with cheers. Barrington (Mark Wing-Davey) and I (as Owen) stayed out for the 'For he's a jolly good fellow' for Rushton and Grinder, and we both felt extreme disgust, but stayed quiet. Then Grinder made his speech, attacking the socialists, which the men enjoyed, goading us to speak. Suddenly, Barrington rose and began his defence. Slowly, carefully, with the strength of suppressed rage. The evening became electric. Everyone remained silent – perhaps too silent. The defence was clear, powerful. I was deeply moved and, towards the end, was able to look around, with some pride in my beliefs as Owen.

At the end, Crass broke in with 'No more speech-making' and the singing began. He sang the Tory work song 'Work Boys Work . . .' which everyone bar the socialists joined in happily. I was angry with Philpott (Kenny Ireland) and Semi-Drunk (Peter-Hugo Daly), who had expressed some socialist leanings, for not realising what they were doing.

Then Mrs Payne (Harriet Walter) stepped forward to sing 'Who Will Buy My Flowers?', accompanied by Semi-Drunk on the piano. This was a sentimental Victorian song which, in rehearsals, we had all done cod crying to, but now there was none of that. The reality of this song moved us all – I felt it was a good description of all our states, and if only we listened, people would change, others were genuinely moved at what before seemed only trite pathos. We joined in the chorus and the harmonies felt beautiful. It was the first moment of real beauty in the evening.

Semi-Drunk tried to sing 'Put Me Among the Girls' and was shouted down (he had in fact started the singing with 'Old Bull and Bush'). Then, accompanied by Barrington on a £3000 violin the college had found, Payne (Bruce Alexander) sang 'Don't Go Out Tonight, Dear Father', a song which no one could take seriously, which went on and on as intended in the book. But it was cod, it was too acted, i.e. a man singing badly and boringly – a dreary song with gestures. Our reactions as a group, instead of being spontaneous and diverse, were calculated and forced. Philpott then sang 'The

Roast Beef of Old England', forgetting almost all the words (quite genuinely) much to the amusement of the lads. Crass rounded off with a political comic song, 'Two Lovely Black Eyes' in which we all joined the chorus.

This then was the end of the songs we had rehearsed. According to the book we should now have gone outside to play games, walk round the grounds, etc. Instead, the evening took an unexpected course, led off by the warmth of Fred's personality. After a pause, he suddenly began to sing a Geordie song, in one of the loveliest voices I ever heard. Quietly, individually, others began to sing, moving somewhere along the dividing line between character and their own identity (gradually letting their characters drift away from them, slowly revealing the group as a group of actors). I forget now the songs that were sung, but everything moved quietly, unforced, from one to the next, some funny, some gentle – nothing boisterous, nothing disruptive, no one shouting anyone down. Just the group enjoying and relishing the talents of its fellow members. Ken stood up and did a monologue for the North (as Bill and I could not think of anything) of the little lad who gets ate by the lion. The waitresses sang a First World War song, beautifully, and one of them recited a monologue. Scottish songs were sung, and the hymns we had sung in rehearsal – 'The Living Stream' and 'Work, for the Night is Coming' were sung so beautifully I felt like crying. Peter-Hugo played two of his compositions on the piano. Mark sang two revolutionary modern songs from a musical on Carpenter. Peter Hartwell did a Canadian song. During all this Hunter stayed in character, suddenly leaping up to sing the National Anthem. At first, he was paid lip service to by the men, led by Crass, and tried to sing the first line of a song, demanding that the men joined in. We let him carry on on his own until he could remember no more. He would return to his seat, jump again, stumble out a few demented, drunken words, and collapse back. No one minded. He was ignored, powerless, the men were together. What significance did he have? He was just a sad, black clown. The company accepted him without malice, stripping him of power. It was the most telling image of the night. The pauses in between songs and monologues were silent, reverential, full of warmth. I went to the lav at one point and missed what was apparently another high spot. Pressure had been put on Fred the carpenter to do a number representing the South. He refused, and Peter-Hugo stood up and, quietly, without a trace of cockney, recited a Thomas Hardy poem. Everyone was thunderstruck. This, if possible, was topped by Pete the paint, who suddenly broke into a song about Plymouth and Drake, in a beautiful bass voice, managing about six verses before he forgot it. It didn't matter. We all now were one group.

Eventually, in one last attempt to gain control, Hunter discovered a ball and led us all out into the spreading darkness on the lawn, to play ball games. All characters bar his were now gone. We stood in the beauty of the trees, as he disappeared across the lawn, clutching onto a young waitress, her white half hidden by his black as they faded across the lawn.

At home, we discussed with Bill the night's happenings. He is over the moon with it. So am I. How can we use it? Got to sleep around 3.00, but awoke at 5.00 feeling less than well, staggering around the place. Had visions of blood poisoning (of the alcoholic type). Decided to go on the waggon for a bit.

There's a play here somewhere.

Stephen Lowe
(Edited extract from *Letters from a Workshop*,
Dartington Theatre Papers, 1979)

*Titles in the
Methuen Modern Plays series
are listed overleaf.*

Dario Fo	
Franca Rame	*The Open Couple & An Ordinary Day*
Michael Frayn	*Balmoral*
	Benefactors
	Jamie On A Flying Visit & Birthday
	Look Look
	Noises Off
Max Frisch	*Andorra*
	The Fire Raisers
Peter Handke	*Kaspar*
	The Long Way Round
	Offending the Audience & Self-Accusation
Kaufman & Hart	*Once in a Lifetime, You Can't Take It With You & The Man Who Came to Dinner*
Barrie Keeffe	*Barbarians*
	Wild Justice, Not Fade Away & Gimme Shelter
John Lahr	*Diary of a Somebody*
Stephen Lowe	*Touched*
John McGrath	*The Cheviot, the Stag and the Black, Black Oil*
David Mamet	*American Buffalo*
	Glengarry Glen Ross
	A Life in the Theatre
	The Shawl & Prairie du Chien
	Speed-the-Plow
David Mercer	*No Limits to Love*
Arthur Miller	*The American Clock*
	The Archbishop's Ceiling
	Danger: Memory!
	The Golden Years & The Man Who Had All the Luck
	Two-Way Mirror
Percy Mtwa	
Mbongeni Ngema }	*Woza Albert!*
Barney Simon	
Tom Murphy	*Too Late for Logic*
	A Whistle in the Dark & Other Plays